Margaret Thatcher

The Iron Lady Who Made History - Biography

(Dead Sheep the Downfall of Margaret Thatcher a Play)

Mistie Carleton

Published By **Simon Dough**

Mistie Carleton

Margaret Thatcher: The Iron Lady Who Made History - Biography (Dead Sheep the Downfall of Margaret Thatcher a Play)

ISBN   978-1-998769-34-6

No part of this guidebook shall be reproduced in any form without permission in writing from the publisher except in the case of brief quotations embodied in critical articles or reviews.

Legal & Disclaimer

The information contained in this ebook is not designed to replace or take the place of any form of medicine or professional medical advice. The information in this ebook has been provided for educational & entertainment purposes only.

The information contained in this book has been compiled from sources deemed reliable, and it is accurate to the best of the Author's knowledge; however, the Author cannot guarantee its accuracy and validity and cannot be held liable for any errors or omissions. Changes are periodically made to this book. You must consult your doctor or get professional medical advice before using any of the suggested remedies, techniques, or information in this book.

Upon using the information contained in this book, you agree to hold harmless the Author from and against any damages, costs, and expenses, including any legal fees potentially resulting from the application of any of the information provided by this guide. This disclaimer applies to any damages or injury caused by the use and application, whether directly or indirectly, of any advice or information presented, whether for breach of contract, tort, negligence, personal injury, criminal intent, or under any other cause of action.

You agree to accept all risks of using the information presented inside this book. You need to consult a professional medical practitioner in order to ensure you are both able and healthy enough to participate in this program.

Table Of Contents

Chapter 1: Change and Decay all Around I See

Without recalling the despairing mood into which Britain fell by 1974's end, it is difficult for Margaret Thatcher to explain how she was able to grab Ted Heath as the Conservative party leader.

Ted Heath suffered two defeats in the general elections of that year. But he was still widely recognized as the leader of the Conservative Party, a dominant figure within British politics. He was the backbencher of whom Mrs Thatcher was most impressed, as well as when she was his Education secretary.

Heath did not see and correctly discerned that the post-war, corporatist British consensus in British politics was falling into disrepute.

Forty-years after those dark days, Londoners still worry about overcrowding. The capital attracts migrants from Europe and the rest of the world; South Kensington is filled with French refugees fleeing Francois Hollande's socialist regime.

1974 saw a heightened sense of anxiety as London's population began to shrink. The result was that many people fled from poor transport, increasing crime, and a general lack of opportunities. As the rich and ambitious sought out opportunities and less severe taxation rates, they moved to the outside suburbs, into provincial towns and even abroad.

Long lines formed at the Commonwealth High Commission offices in London for hopeful emigrants. The number of applications to Canada and Australia in

1974 increased more than 50% compared to previous years.

Many white-collar workers abandoned Britain. In 1975, almost 30.000 Britons emigrated from Britain to South Africa. This was despite the uncertainty about the political stability of the apartheid system. 85,000 people left the UK in 1975 than arrived, leading to a drop in the population for the first record.

Britain had more internationally acclaimed actors and musicians than any other country, but they could not afford to leave the UK. They pay 83% income tax and 98% investment tax. The Rolling Stones were faced with huge tax bills due to their royalties and decided to move to France in 1969. Rod Steward and David Bowie emigrated to America between 1974-75. Elton John was a star of 1975. He sold 28 million records that year.

According to The Daily Express, which at the time chronicled the entire exodus of the wealthy and famous by tracing every development, he only kept a few pennies of every pound from royalties and investments.

Douglas Hurd (Heath's political secretary) and a Tory 'Wet, recorded in his journal: "All of the mechanics that life crumbling around me - heating.

Travelling abroad by Britons was restricted in terms of the amount they could carry with them to help protect their nation's diminishing reserves. The media's portrayal that their country was the "sick man" of Europe was accurate when these travelers returned to Britain. The strike was everywhere; polls indicated that there was a deep sense in the nation of national pessimism. It also suggested that Britain's problems would not be solved.

Denis Thatcher (an experienced businessman who quit Burmah Oil to become a father) told Carol, his daughter, that the unions controlled the country. "The unions were always on strike which was a failure for nationalised industries. They had a monopoly. The dockers were a terrible menace. You sent your goods to London but the dockers would not touch them. They were capable to hold the country captive, and they did.

Alan Clark, Conservative diarist was concerned about his declining stock market portfolio. In November 1974, he felt "doom and foreboding" because of the probability of another Arab/Israeli war, total collapse of industry, etc. (not to mention the 'Nuclear Exchange ')".).

Although the Berlin Wall was erected 15 years prior, no one believed that there would be an end to Cold War US-Soviet.

Alan Clark was not the first to predict that there would be another Yom Kippur war in October 1973. Not that the United States, with its Watergate woes, was able to enforce order and stability in an unstable global world.

In Britain, this was an era of de-industrialisation, of under-investment in business, of balance of payments crises, of strikes and power cuts and three-day weeks to conserve dwindling fuel stocks, and of crippling inflation and punitive marginal tax rates. The heads of nationalised industries who were not in control gave way to the above-inflation wage rises for militant trade union leaders. Jack Jones, Joe Gormley, and Arthur Scargill were well-known names.

Every word they spoke was reported in newspapers, which had two or three full-time labor correspondents. While the Labour party was at the helm, it was almost required that they comply with the demands from their union barons and paymasters. The Tories, however, were much more indulgent.

"This was an era," Lord Tebbit stated in a December 2014 interview with the author. "When the Tory party leaders saw their role merely as to remove the rough edges from the work of previous Labour governments."

There was no way out of the country's mess. William Whitelaw was the Tory thought to be Ted Heath's successor. Tebbit points to his deep commitment to the party's philosophy at the time. He believed that politics was moving steadily left and there is no way to fix it.

Although Labour party was able to keep the loyalty of public sector workers, unionized workers in the declining strike-bound industries and the unionized workers, the aspirant upper- and lower-middle class were looking for a new beginning.

This attitude reflected a suppressed anger among British business leaders and entrepreneurs at Britain's post-war destruction.

At that time, no British politician would dare challenge the Keynesian economic consensus of post-war and take on vested interests groups, especially unions in nationalized industries. This was despite all the evidence of Britain's economic failure facing the governing class.

British retail prices rose 19% and wage rates increased by a shocking 29%

between 1974-75. Despite all this industrial blackmail, the industrial total production fell by 3 percent. Each of these measures reflect a postwar record.

Britain had lost most its former empire within the first post-war period but was still far away from finding a role and any will to project hard power or soft power overseas. The constant stream of Irish Republican terrorist attack in Ulster and elsewhere on British soil meant that the Army was still professionally trained. Britain did not act like it was taking its place in the world.

The Defence Secretary Roy Mason observed that the Permanent secretary did not arrive at the office when Turkey invaded Cyprus in July 1974. It was a strategically vital island that held two British military bases.

Mason went to the office on his own, but was unable to use the scrambler telephone due to the absence of his civil service employees. Mason was told that he doesn't like coming to work Saturdays, so it was impossible to summon a private secretary with a master key.

A look at newspapers dating back to 1974 confirms the idea of a country and a world that are about to fall into chaos.

The bomb placed on a bus bound for Catterick by the Irish Republican Army (IRA), killed 12 family members and servicemen in February. At the time, there were approximately 200 Ulster terrorist deaths each year. There were many more people injured.

Newspapers of that time show wider cultural shifts. It was during this time, regardless of exchange controls, that the

British began to take regular trips abroad, drinking more wine and less beer, as well as switching their loyalty to foreign goods.

Datsun marketed its Cherry as Britain's best-selling import car, at a moment when Austins Triumphs and domestically made Fords were failing to fulfill the needs British motorists. Cherry cost PS1,055 which is about PS9,000.500 today. The Cherry's advertisements were very simple and uninspiring. "And what are you getting is a car shaped car with real car looks and car-sized performances," the ad helped to explain to those who weren't quite sure what they were looking at.

A packet of 20 Extra Mild could cost 29 pence. This is equivalent to PS2.65 in modern money. However, Embassy King size was priced at a premium at 36 pence. That's PS3.25 today. Benson & Hedge's is the contemporary equivalent of Embassy King Size. A smoker could expect to pay approximately PS8.50 for a 2015 purchase. This is due in part to successive Chancellors increasing'sin tax'.

It is astonishing to see the drop in prices for consumer electronic products, such as TVs and music systems. The price of the basic Sinclair Cambridge pocket-calculator, which includes only four functions and a carrying case, was shockingly high at PS12.95. For a fraction of the price, you could find a better machine on the high streets today.

Building societies were eager to get deposits from savers, and they advertised rates as high as 13 or 14 percent. Today's disappointed savers were surprised at how generous these interest rates seemed. However, with inflation at around 20%, it was actually a negative rate. Thatcher's charm was in large part due to the inability for people, especially pensioners to protect their savings from the ravages caused by inflation.

You can also see how little Britain has evolved in other ways. There was an acute concern about educational standards, and in October 1974 the Daily Mail reported that Oxford had set "easy exam questions" to encourage entry into comprehensive schools. The grammar school students are given more difficult questions than the public school pupils. This was even in the days before comprehensive education orthodoxy. There were concerns that bright working-class kids were being left behind because of the dissolution of grammar schools.

Britain seemed to be in a sad place, barely at ease with its surroundings. Six days later, the Catterick outrage was overturned by coal miners who went on strike in protest at their 30 per cent pay demand. Three days later Alexander Solzhenitsyn, a Moscow resident, was expelled. Ted Heath's Conservative regime lost power to Harold Wilson's Labour party the final day of February. He had effectively asked the electorate which British ruler they wanted. Britain decided that it was not him.

In many other ways, the summer remained chaotic and bewilderingly chaotic. In August, President Richard Nixon was forced from office over Watergate. However, Wilson gained an overall majority of only three seats in the British election in October. This came just days after IRA Bombs killed five people in Guildford and injured 65.

John Stonehouse, Labour's MP for the South, disappeared on a Miami Beach beach in November. He was later captured in Australia with a fake passport. Two more IRA bombings of pubs in Birmingham killed 21 more people. In the ensuing 24 hours, parliament passed The Prevention of Terrorism Act. This gave police the ability to detain terrorist suspects and ban them off the mainland for five days. The end of an extremely worrying year was marked by Israel's announcement in December that they had the necessary means to make nuclear weapons.

Chapter 2: Heath Will Murder Your

Denis Thatcher's husband was shocked when Margaret Thatcher revealed to him in late 1974 that she planned on challenging for the Conservative party leadership. He stated to Margaret

Thatcher, "You must be mad." "You don't have a chance. Heath will murder.

Carol was then told by him, "Ofcourse, she told me I would support all her way." "That is what marriage all about... Ofcourse, if she wasn't going to lose, I had nothing to be concerned about."

Ted Heath (the man she hoped would be her successor as leader) was just as strident. He said to her "If necessary" when she went to his House of Commons offices to tell him. "You will be lost."

Journalists and MPs alike shared her profound doubts about her prospects. It was often based upon a puerile class hostility which infects British politics now and then.

"Margaret's pure Surbiton [a notoriously dull London suburb] in all of its glory and that won't be enough for me," stated Ian Gilmour MP. Gilmour is frequently referred to as a Tory giant. Gilmour, a 3rd-baronet educated at Eton College and Balliol College Oxford, was completely unaware of the fact Thatcher's "ordinary" origins are the reason she appealed directly to large parts of the electorate.

Derek Marks, a writer for the Daily Express, was critical of the Conservative party's support. He dismissed her as "totally out-of-touch with anyone except carefully corseted and middle-class women".

The mid 1970s gender stereotypes were perfectly matched by the class prejudices of the Cynics. Woodrow Wyatt, who became a sycophantic Thatcherite later, dismissed her in Labour-supporting Sunday Mirror. He called her "a limited, bossy and self-righteous woman", a language that he certainly wouldn't have used for a male politician. It was even stranger than the lack of confidence among the cynics in her prospects that Mrs Thatcher believed a woman would not break through to lead any major British political party.

When she was asked if her desire to become the first woman prime minister, she replied "No" to the Finchley Press in her constituency. "There will never be a female prime minister in mine lifetime. The male population has too much prejudiced." Actually, the true truth is that the truly obstructive areas of sexist or snobbish resistance are less prevalent in the general election than they were in Westminster, and especially the Tory Party.

Even men who were drawn by Thatcher's Right wing outlook and middle class instincts were cautious of supporting a female candidate. Norman Tebbit said that he had only spoken to her about the need to replace Ted Heath in the Conservative leadership. They had not met in the tearoom. Tebbit did not particularly interest in education. She had been Heath's Secretary of State. "I'm honest, I thought that a woman leading the party would be a handicap. Tebbit, who now resides in Bury St Edmonds in active retirement, recalled that if there was a convincing male candidate we would have all gone for him.

Norman Tebbit is an observant who can see the changes in fortunes within Conservative party. However, he underestimated Thatcher's chances to be able to take into account both her luck as well as her pluck.

Conservative philosophers believed Thatcher had been a terrible Education Secretary. Thatcher's tenure at the Ministry of Education was notable for one controversial, radical move. Thatcher removed one day of school milk for every child. Protestors then chanted "Thatcher The Milk Snatcher."

A proud product of a rigorous grammar-school education, she failed to reverse its assault on academic selection. In fact more grammar schools were shut down under her watch than under the Secretary of State.

*

An early election was initiated by coal miners voting four to one in favor of a strike in January. This led to an intensification of industrial anarchy. Heath travelled to the country on Thursday 28th February 1974. The unions' intransigence had caused Heath to be defeated. The Conservatives claimed to be the party that would bring industrial relations back to normal, but they were rebuffed. It was depressing, as Thatcher noted later. "We had finally come to terms with the unions and people had not supported me." This lesson was to be learned later. Tories had to present a more comprehensive appeal to those who would like to move beyond the postwar corporatist consensus.

Although no leader could claim a clear win, the prime minster was the clear loser. Labour polled slightly lower than the Conservatives (37.1 per cent versus 37.9), but it was still the largest party with only 301 seats to 297 for the Tories. The Liberals' performance was particularly impressive, reflecting widespread disenchantment towards the two main parties. They received nearly

20% of the vote - six millions votes. But because they used the first past-the-post voting system, the Liberals tended to cause damage to the Conservatives, rather than making a breakthrough. And they finished with just 14 seats.

Heath may have quit immediately after such a repudiation. However, it was never his way to be easy. He spent 72 hours negotiating a Con-Lib pact. The idea was to keep Downing Street open to the possibility, but he finally had to concede the inevitable. On the Monday after, March 4th, he called a final Cabinet. The meeting was depressing despite the fact that 10 Downing Street was overflowing with flowers from friends and well-wishers. The atmosphere was bizarre, not least because the Prime minister refused to acknowledge that the defeat in the election was anything but a temporary setback that would be swiftly reversed. Later, some in the Cabinet were shocked that Thatcher had decided to mark the end of their shared experience as government. One presenter said she made a point to talk "in emotional terms" about the amazing experience of team loyalty that she felt was shared since 1970 when the Conservatives were elected.

A lot of people saw her unabashed disdain for the inadequacies, and even its vacillation, as evidence of her dishonesty. Others sympathize more with her and suggested that this was simply a reflection on how well mannered she had been raised by Grantham's father. It's also possible that she was grateful at the time to Heath and that her antipathy towards him, and what he stood up for, only took root towards end of the year that the Tories were out.

Many of her colleagues were convinced that her conversion to the cause monetarism/free market was so abrupt and insincere.

Whatever one's interpretation of the intervention, Heath knew on Monday after Thursday's election that even though he could not hold onto office, it was obvious to him. He was taken to Buckingham Palace where he resigned. The Queen invited Harold Wilson, who was then to form a government that would be inherently unstable because of its lack for an overall majority. Thatcher was aware that the Tories' defeat had not resolved anything. "I knew that it was not time for a change to government but for a shift in the Conservative Party."

Thatcher had begun to think about how to bring this revolution to fruition.

*

After the February elections, Westminster assumed Harold Wilson would just wait and see if the right moment came to hold a second poll to secure the majority he required to govern. Even for those who couldn't hide their disgust for Heath, this created a sense of discipline in Conservative MPs.

The core problem of the new Conservative opposition, however, was its lack economic credibility. It had produced a manifesto that was to be used for the 1970 general election. This manifesto marked a shift towards a more liberal market approach from the corporatist consensus. They were again confronted by the ferocity and anarchy of industrial anarchy once they were back in office. Heath then drifted back to a de facto strategy for industrial operations. The Tory government faced striking and unreasonable pay demands from the dockers and car workers, as well as the most dangerously from the coal miners.

Heath made a bold move in 1972 and ordered a unilateral 90 days freeze on prices and rents. Thatcher, as a cabinet member, took collective responsibility for this volte faced, even though she did not have an economic portfolio.

Charles Moore, in his authorized biography, argues that Thatcher did not join a Right-wing Tory party of MPs who intellectually disapproved Heath's corporatist tendencies. Furthermore, there is no evidence that Thatcher ever spoke out against Heath when she was in cabinet. The free market Economic

Dining Club was formed by a group dissidents to oppose Heath. Enoch Powell was one of its members, as were Nicholas Ridley, John Nott and Cecil Parkinson. Thatcher was not part of it, partly because some of them feared that a female member would bring down the clubby atmosphere. Thatcher was, however, not seen as a political thinker in her early 70s. Her style of politics in those days was not intellectual. She was anti-intellectual even. Instead, her politics were personal and practical. Although she did not support the government being able to impose income caps and prices, she was not opposed in principle. It was clear that she had reservations about it in principle. She argued in favor of its eventual elimination when the cabinet considered quietly scrapping it.

Her Right-wing instincts on other subjects were more evident. Because she represented Finchley, which has a large Jewish population, she was an outspoken defender Israel. She was fiercely critical of the general Arabist orientation of cabinet members and advocated for Israel during Yom Kippur in October 1973. She was hawkish even at the time on Irish Republican terrorism. If Dublin allowed the IRA safe passage south of its border, she voted in favor of retaliation.

*

Following the February defeat in February, there was widespread discontent about Heath. Not just among Right-wing critics. Hugh Fraser, then married with Lady Antonia Fraser started to position himself as a challenger to Heath. Fraser was never taken seriously by anyone, except possibly his wife. His half-hearted moves were an indication of the trouble Heath was in with the parliamentary party.

William Whitelaw, Heath's Northern Ireland Secretary was considered the natural successor. But there were concerns that Whitelaw was too indecisive or wishy-washy after a long spell in Ulster.

Geoffrey Howe, Robert Carr and Robert Carr, both of whom had been employed at Employment and the Home Office respectively, were also mentioned.

They were all considered to be serious runners. Even the plotters who were always determined Heath had to go. Airey Neave is the most prominent of these, having been MP for Abingdon since 1953.

Neave, who maintained close relationships with British intelligence service personnel long after the war, was a clever and understated man who preferred working in the background. He was centre-right in the party but was not an ideologue. His main interest in politics was British science advancement. Thatcher's scientific heritage was something he loved. She also maintained an interest for science even after she entered politics full-time. This was one such moment in British history, when many of the most highly trained scientists fled the country for better work elsewhere. Thatcher was also concerned by Neave's concern that British industry was unable to offer ambitious scientists and engineers the opportunities available elsewhere.

Neave was adamantly against Heath since 1959, when Heath became ill and forced him to resign from his junior position at Harold Macmillan's government. Heath, who was then chief whip, said to Neave that Heath was "finished" but Heath later denied it.

Whatever the truth may be, Heath didn't make any effort to support a man whose political career had been cut short. Neave might have received a consolation knighthood, which would have been standard for a Tory with a very successful war behind him. It could have kept Heath onside, and possibly prevented Heath's downfall.

Neave was open to throwing his weight and all his contacts within the party behind anyone who could possibly dislodge Heath. His problem in the spring 1974 was that there was no plausible candidate.

May was boiling over. Neave saw Heath for a separate matter. She noted that Heath's leader was in a "v. Neave was poor, with red eyes, too fat, and feeling depressed. Heath should be able to see that Heath's off-putting appearance was caused by a thyroid disorder. Neave's only hope of a party escape was that Heath would be persuaded to appoint Whitelaw. Neave, along with his accomplices, knew Heath would not abandon without a fight. Harold Wilson, meanwhile, could pick the moment when a Tory leadership fight could be called to call an election to secure a working majority.

After losing power in the February election, some Conservative Party members were forced to think critically about the events and to challenge Heath on intellectual and strategic grounds. Sir

Keith Joseph was to be the key figure in this process, not Margaret Thatcher.

Joseph and Thatcher both served in Heath's cabinet, until February 1974 when they were defeated. This disappointed the intellectual Right and the emerging monetarist thinkers. They had both spent heavily in their respective Departments, he at Health, she was at Education, but neither of them did much to challenge political orthodoxy. Joseph was more than Thatcher in that he began to think about ways out of this quagmire. He also explored radical ideas, such as privatisation promoted at the Institute of Economic Affairs. Simultaneously a group influential economic journalists, led Samuel Brittan at Financial Times and Peter Jay by the Times, began to promote a "monetarist" approach for controlling inflation via control of money supply.

Joseph was the leader for this group of revolutionary MPs. Joseph, an Oxford-educated fellow, was also a member in good standing of All Souls. He was not a gifted intellectual, but was unworldly. His "gaffes" were often nothing more than a way of speaking the truth in a sloppy manner. He never took much pleasure in plotting against the leader of his party. Neave on the other hand, who was positioning him as kingmaker, felt a personal hate for Heath. Joseph understood that his request for a change in leadership was an intellectual recognition by the Tories of their failure to recognize a reef.

Thatcher at that point was just a supporter and a close friend in Joseph's tentative challenges towards Heath. But, Shecher began to love him and her husband was excited about it. Carol told Denis, her father, that she had said and kept to it that he was England's greatest man. "He had a large influence on Margaret. He was kind [and] he had complete integrity." Joseph was Jewish, something that might have upset many Tory luminaries back then. Margaret Thatcher didn't share the anti-Semitism of some of her party members and, throughout her career many of her closest confidantes were Jewish.

Heath could have made Thatcher shadow Chancellor of Exchequer to help with the "Keith Joseph problem" and put him on the mast of collective accountability. Heath wasn't able to make this gesture and instead named Robert Carr, an arch-traditional Tory "wet" to the key portfolio. Thatcher was first moved to Environment and then became Carr's deputy. While it was unsatisfactory and odd, it was the compromise that allowed her to shine in Parliament, at least compared with her low-key boss who was often poorly prepared.

Slowly, Joseph began examining the limits of the extent to which he could critique the prevailing economic orthodoxy. However, he was not seen as being able to attack Heath's leadership. He then set out to give speeches all over the country on past Tory mistakes and economic policy. Joseph was prepping the ground for One Nation conservatism. This is what Heath's supporters know well.

*

Joseph noted in June 1974 that the successive "Conservative Governments" after World War Two had, for understandable reasons not considered it possible to reverse the large majority of the Socialism-accumulating debris which they discovered each time they returned to power. We built upon it instead. I'm responsible for following too many of its trends.

That self-criticism wasn't just applicable to Margaret Thatcher but was also directed at Heath and the rest of the Conservative hierarchy. Joseph made waves in Preston during the second general elections of the year. In September, he challenged the most important post-war economic shibboleth: the idea that full employment was the primary goal for good government. "So, we made up a belief that these gaunt, tight, men in caps, and mufflers were around the corner. And so, we tailored our policies to fit these imaginary conditions. They were indeed imaginary.

This angered Heath, as it suggested to Labour that the Tories were really indifferent towards unemployment and the wider conditions of what was then known as the working-man.

*

Keith Joseph's Preston speech had a huge impact partly because everyone was made aware that there was an anti Heath insurgency. The entire speech was printed in its entirety in the Times. It was also widely reported in other newspapers. The speech clearly showed that the insurgents were determined not to accept the failures of incomes and trade union deals, but the targeting inflation via monetarist ideas as the mainstay of Tory policy.

Ironically, Thatcher as Heath's Environment shadow spokeswoman was actually embracing a series interventionsist policies that were designed to win 1974's second general elections.

Tories desperately needed eye-catching initiatives in order to win over the middle class, who felt oppressed due to inflation and couldn't maintain their living standard in the same way that manual workers could with their powerful trade union protectors. Thatcher signed a deal with some hesitation to help subsidise the mortgage interest rate. In effect, Thatcher applied an entirely arbitrary and anti-free marketplace mechanism to homeowners, guaranteeing that their payments would not exceed the random rate of nine, a half percent.

Even though the Tories lost their October election and Harold Wilson got his working majority (just 4 seats), Margaret Thatcher was considered one of the Tory stars. She had effectively established herself as the most compelling alternative should Heath fail to succeed.

Chapter 3: The Personal is All

Heath was defeated in two consecutive election defeats, which exacerbated opposition from the Parliamentary party. Many on the backbenches had long resent his soggy centrist policies, but few believed that Heath would ever win another general election.

Heath rejected any suggestions from even close allies that he might consider stepping down. Heath would almost certainly have supervised the succession of his leader, Willie Whitelaw, if he had not forced himself to do so. Whitelaw was a strict politician with old-fashioned notions that loyalty and would not even consider challenging his leader. In those days, the Conservative Party was strongly attached to the current leadership, regardless of its ineffectiveness. This was clearly reflected in the pages that comprised the Daily Telegraph, the Conservative Party's house magazine. Many of the Telegraph's most notable writers, such John O'Sullivan (TE Utley), Frank Johnson (Frank Johnson), were firmly in Thatcher's camp - they even helped her with speeches and acted as informal advisers. The Telegraph as an institution tended not to get involved in the debate, and remained neutral. It generally supported the Conservative leader at the time, however, but it was not a part of the fray.

Douglas Hurd, an old friend of Heath's even after he became an MP, explained to the author how Heath could have handled a leadership challenge better.

Hurd stated that Hurd believed he, and only he, could bring the country back to its feet. Heath took the fact Labour had not won a majority of over a handful to be evidence of his strong performance as leader. Hurd was also among his allies. He told Hurd that he must continue to lead the Conservative campaign for the Yes vote in the referendum on Britain joining the European Common Market. Heath was confident that he would win the leadership battle, which became increasingly likely.

"I believed Ted was capable of winning, but only if Ted struck an entirely new note, a conciliatory one, saying that his attention would be more focused on the parliamentary party. That was the problem with him. He didn't get along with people and they resented his approach. It was a kind of arrogance from his part." Even though he believed

Heath would survive, Hurd privately doubted whether he would become Prime minister again.

Thatcher was also shocked by the lackluster analysis of Tory benches concerning the party's prospects under Heath. She assumed the party will be welcomed back after Labour had been deemed to have ruined Britain's economy. In her autobiography, she said that too many Tory wishful tinkers believed that the Conservative Party might be able to return to power with a mandate from a doctor. Ted was sure of his own medical credentials.

Heath was always concerned about his personal aspects.

Airey Neave almost certainly wouldn't have dedicated his political energies in 1974 for unseating Heath if not for Heath's casual comment, that his political career was "finished", as he had stated above.

*

Hurd, who shared Heath's "wet" Tory outlook and was fond of Heath, confirms this. Heath was a close book, even for those who spent long hours by his side in Parliament.

"Somehow within the first months of his becoming Prime Minister [in 1969], he had lost that sensibility to people he showed when he were chief whip." Even his political enemies admitted that while chief whip he spent too much time with backbench politicians who had experienced personal problems with drink or women. This made it difficult for him to support the government in drafting contentious legislation.

His premiership was a triumphant moment for humanity, perhaps due to his isolation in high office.

Thatcher was struck too and recorded the Heathite trait in an autobiography. It is possible, however, that she was retrospectively identifying Heathite's failures to justify her challenge to his leadership.

"He might be willing to admit and learn from government's mistakes. He might have invited skilled backbench criticisms to join him in Shadow speaking on his behalf and to help with policy rethinking. He could have changed the Shadow Cabinet's complexion to be more representative of parliamentary opinion.

She was particularly upset by Heath's promotion of his acolytes Michael Heseltine & Paul Channon, who couldn't hide their contempt towards Conservatives like Margaret Thatcher.

Hurd says Heath had eight to nine platonic friends, with whom Heath could go out to dinner and the opera, but his life was extremely lonely.

He was not gay, but the truth of the matter is that he didn't have a lot of time for women. He had been deeply devoted and loved his mother. I don't think that he had high regard for [Thatcher].

Interestingly, Thatcher was not a part of Hurd's conviction Heath was not homosexual. WFDeedes, editor of Daily Telegraph, took note of Thatcher's private conversation in 1976. M seems convinced that TH has a homosexual mind. (Women have more precise instincts than us. I said it in charitably, "an instinct sublimated on boats!"

Thatcher, in her memoirs claimed that she felt some sympathy towards Heath after the October general electoral defeat. "I felt sorry about Ted Heath personally. He had his music and his small circle of friends but politics was his whole life." She clearly considered him a classic sad bachelor. His poor judgments were not corrected by the presence at his side of a good lady, much as Douglas Hurd felt.

Thatcher also mentioned a personal reason for Heath's pain in the same entry. He had been through some personal setbacks before that year. Heath's godson was one of those who had lost.

Heath's circle if mature female friends gave him chaste companionship. But, certainly, not intimacy. Hurd isn't doubtful that a "sensible" woman would have been a great help.

Hurd asserts that he never saw any evidence of Heath's early animosity with Thatcher. Heath was able to offend Airey Neave. However, there wasn't that kind of personal hatred with Thatcher. "She was loyal during her time in the cabinet. I didn't know of any significant quarrels when I worked at number 10. "I never believed he cared about her. But the anger came later."

Thatcher was in some ways in awe when Heath appeared. Hurd says, "She was actually afraid of Ted at that stage because he wasn't predictable. He was capable of launching into a tirade. She carefully listened to what she said and was constantly worried about Ted's intentions.

Hurd states that Airey Neave (Thatcher's facilitator) was someone he took "with a pinch" of salt. He didn't wear his heart on the sleeve and it was a complex challenge to find where his heart lies.

*

Norman Tebbit disliked Heath personally and disagreed with him on nearly all political points. But, Tebbit also believes that Heath's personal flaws were key to his downfall. Tebbit didn't believe Heath could be described as psychologically inept, and was unable to "reach out" to backbenchers and make them feel valued.

Tebbit recalls: "Having lost the second elections, it was clear that he would be having to go. The problem was who would succeed him." "Willie Whitelaw attended, but he was deeply committed to the philosophy of the party at the moment that politics is moving steadily to the Left and that there is nothing he can do about it."

Edward du Cann, a finance professional with a mixed business history, was more on the Right. He "favored himself as a leader but not too many other people did".

Chapter 4: Sir Sheath Boils It

The anti-Heathite faction, though unsure of his temperament, put their faith in Keith Joseph.

Thatcher was a loyal lieutenant to him in any future leadership challenge, immediately following the October defeat. After three weeks, Keith Joseph was defeated by Heath in an extraordinary act of political selflessness. He intended to use his economic arguments in an expanded discussion about the "tone of national living" at a speech in Edgbaston 19 October. He called for a battle of ideas in all schools, universities, publications, committees, TV studios, to oppose the prevailing collectivist views. He had taken part of his argument form papers from the Left-wing Child Poverty Action Group. However, it later disavowed the data.

Joseph was frequently referred to in political circles as an ideological Rightwinger. In Harold Macmillan's disingenuous (and famous) words, "The only boring Jew i have ever known" Joseph, who was raised with money and suffered from self-loathing, actually had a strong social conscience. As a child, he would take food from the family house in Chelsea to feed the street begging.

While his intentions were sound in the Edgbaston speech, they were absurd and decorous in his language. He stated that the balance of our people, our human stock, was at risk because many children were born to unmarried, low-intelligence, and most importantly, very low educated women. Joseph, a fellow of All Souls, made his remarks even more irritating. Worse yet, he suggested to Private Eye that the NHS need to equip these young women using contraception to safeguard the national gene pools.

Enoch Powell seemed to delight in Joseph's shame six years before he was fired by Heath over his speech entitled 'Rivers of Blood. He said laconically that it was great fun to see another person get in trouble for a speech. "I almost wondered, if the River Tiber was getting ready to roll again."

Joseph's ineptitude caused so much panic that even his close friends thought he couldn't stand up against Heath. Airey Neave recorded in his diary, "He was very tactless. This has raised a storm. This will affect his chances to replace Heath." Neave hoped that Heath would be helped by the row. He "seems back to his position. I suppose we must accept the worst."

Heath appeared to have found his balance again after suffering two defeats in succession. Heath took this time to reshuffle his shadow-cabinet team in order to confuse his rivals. He was also arguing with backbench 1922 about the need for new rules for its leadership election. Given her performance and experience in Shadow Cabinet, It was quite insulting to place Thatcher in number two on his Treasury team. But she didn't give up, and she accepted the challenge. Her role was to strengthen her position as chief challenger by delivering strong performances in Parliament.

The leadership issue took a dramatic turn when Joseph visited Thatcher to tell him he wouldn't challenge Heath. She recounts the conversation here in her autobiography.

"I am sorry, I just can't run. Since then, the press have been at my door. They have been cruel. Helen [his spouse] can't handle it and I have decided that I just can not stand."

His mind was very clear. I was close to despair. We simply could not leave the Party and country to Ted's style of politics. I remember saying to Keith: "Look Keith. I'm going to stand if you don't want to." Because it is our viewpoint that someone has to stand.

Thatcher's memories of that conversation sound contrived, far-fetched and implausible, even though the general thrust of what Joseph and she discussed was fairly accurate. Charles Moore, a staunch supporter, admitted that it was possible that Mrs Thatcher was not surprised or upset. However, she did admit that it was possible that she may have gotten wind that Joseph was about to quit.

Denis asked her if she was going for it and she responded, "You must be out your mind, there is no hope."

Thatcher knew that she had a chance with her campaign if she gained the full trust of Airey Neave. Keith Joseph handed her the baton but he had never built a campaign team. Even late in the autumn, Neave was still trying to persuade Edward du Cann, despite concerns over his business dealings, to oppose Heath.

Yet, there was still some doubt in Tory hearts over choosing a female partner.

Norman Tebbit remembers, "We were really pushed to decide who it should have been." "Airey Negive took me to the side and said, 'It's got have to be Margaret.

Tebbit says that the Labour party assumed in the mid 1970s that if any party were going to have a female leader, it would be the Labour party. "I don't think anyone thought that we were ready for women leaders. While I was not in favor of it, I couldn't imagine the electorate backing it. I believed it would be a significant handicap.

*

Margaret Thatcher's sex led to her hiding other flaws and qualities. Those who were able look past the fact that she was female tend to view her in an English way. They also see her as a product of her small-town life. Alfred Roberts, her dad, was a grocer in Grantham, Lincolnshire. His family lived above his shop. He rose to prominence through his thrift, intelligence, hard work and perseverance. He was elected independent alderman. He also served briefly as mayor and chair of the local Rotary Club. It is an important role in Grantham. Alfred became quite wealthy despite the fact that their lifestyle was modest. They were committed Methodists. Margaret and Muriel, their young sister, would attend Grantham's Weslyan Church three- to four times per Sunday. "We were Methodists," she later explained. "Methodism means method." This may explain Margaret's dislike of frivolity and idleness, which might also explain her lack of sense of humor. Lords Hurd & Tebbit, her former colleagues, still shudder at their memories of explaining jokes or double entendres.

Her childhood was hard and her parents distant, even by current standards. There was no hardship and her childhood is not comparable to that of an American politician.

Margaret, a brilliant girl, won a scholarship for a fee-paying girl to attend grammar school. This was by far the most prestigious school in the area. Alfred received no fees even though Muriel was not awarded a scholarship. Margaret's natural ability to take things seriously was evident at nine when she won a poetry competition at her primary school. When the headmistress complimented Margaret on her luck, she responded clearly: "I was not lucky, I deserved."

She did well at school and was not an outstanding student. Her father had to pay for her tuition at Oxford and her living expenses there after she missed out on a scholarship.

After finishing her Chemistry degree at Somerville College, she behaved in a manner that undergraduates refer to as a "hack". She persevered in her climb up the Oxford University Conservative Association's (OUCA) hierarchy, putting aside the boys of public schools to become president. It was a sure sign that future adult political ambitions were in the making, just as it is now.

Thatcher, who was criticised for her cultural background throughout her entire life, was often ridiculed. She didn't have a passion for literature or theatre and was skeptical about Modernism. However, she did read TS Eliot's poems. Margaret Roberts would have struggled to understand why the second part was so offensive if she had not been called "second-class Chemist" by the principal at Somerville College.

She was proud of having studied and achieved success with something so practical and sensible like chemistry, even though it was sometimes looked down upon by Oxford's majority of undergraduates.

She was surrounded by young careerists from the OUCA who were mostly former schoolboys. These boys arrived at university with more confidence and were easier to socialize with. Margaret Roberts was not invited to Somerville College social dinners, as she "had nothing else to contribute". This was a sneering, and any college academic would see it as their responsibility. Margaret Roberts was shaped by Grantham's narrowness, which was later described as "the most boring village in Britain" by The Sun newspaper.

Despite her comforting, stable, Methodist-provincial upbringing, it was what set her apart, first at Oxford, then later in her rise to the top of the Conservative party.

Lord Tebbit believes you can exaggerate the degree to which the Conservative party was obsessed by class in the 1960s & 1970s. His pedigree was derived from the "back end of Edmonton," which is a poor section of north London. His father went through periods of unemployment in 1930s. Tebbit's later accounts, which were infamous, show that his dad "got onto his bike to find work" rather than rioting as some unemployed people did 50 years later. These standards were positive for Thatcher's childhood.

The key point is that World War Two no longer exists as a living memory.

Tebbit explained to the author, "You might have been at Eton and Sandhurst and the guy on either side of that House might be at Bootle secondary contemporary."

Tebbit could be from the back end in a rough area of London.

Thatcher did not share that male experience from military service, but Tebbit is making a valid point. Many of those successful people were the product of great grammar schools. Thatcher ended up closing many of them when she was Education Secretary. Ted Heath, Harold Wilson, and Ted Heath were fighting in the House of Commons in 1970s. These were battles among two grammar school boys from stable, but not well-off childhoods who eventually found Oxford. 40 years later, Oxbridge, the Oxbridge, and the great, but very expensive, public schools, have tightened their grip on politics, the professions, and on the Arts than ever.

David Cameron, Conservative leader was from Eton and George Osborne, his chancellor had been educated at St Paul's. Boris Johnson (the mayor of London) was an Etonian and Balliol, Oxford. True, Labour leader Ed Miliband attended Haverstock school. This school was once known for being 'Labour's Eton' as it was loved by the Left-wing intelligentsia in Primrose Hill and Hampstead. (His Marxist philosopher father Ralph couldn't have educated his sons privately without making a fuss with his neighbors in north London.

Ed Balls was Labour's shadow chief executive, and was educated privately prior to going to Oxford. Nick Clegg was a leader of the Liberal Democrats and went to Westminster School. He then went on to Cambridge. Nigel Farage, the leader of the UK Independence Party and seen as the natural ally to white van man and who lambasts those he calls the political elite, was educated privately at Dulwich College.

The pitch is not just in politics. In some eyes, the Golden Globes awards for best actor early 2015 were boiled down to a gladiatorial fight between Benedict Cumberbatch, a student at Harrow, and Eddie Redmayne. Redmayne was a close friend of Prince William's from Eton. The Left blames Thatcherism for the inequalities in economic life and laments the dominance of girls and boys from public schools. The explanation is actually simpler. Labour and Conservatives accepted the notion of selection in education as socially divisive during the 1960s to 1970s. They joyfully oversaw the destruction grammar schools. Margaret Thatcher, Ted Heath's Education Secretary, led this effort with more passion than any other. It has meant that only parents with annual incomes of more than PS33,000 are now able to provide a first-class education for their children.

Tebbit saw Thatcher's limitations as her political strength. Tebbit says that "She was always remarkably quiet." Her personality was quite easy to identify. One, she was the child of a Grantham shopkeeper. These were middle-class, lower-ranking, respected people. She was a nonconformist Christian. She was also a scientist. If you can recall these three key parts of her history, you will always have a good idea how she would react when faced with any situation.

Her last asset, which was quite different to Heath's, was a patient companion who would tolerate her oddities and single-minded pursuit for the highest political office. He also made sure she got her back on track when she was in trouble. Tebbit explained that Thatcher had only spoken a few words to Tebbit when she became the leading challenger against Heath. As he got to know Margaret, he started to learn more about her and began to see them at political or social events. Denis simply had to knock on the tabletop and say "come, old lady, it's about time for you to go", and Margaret would follow his lead and pick up her handbag before disappearing into the night.

Chapter 5: Heath's Fall

Although Keith Joseph was forced from the race and Thatcher emerged the obvious challenger to her, few MPs nor political journalists believed she would be able to topple Heath. Hurd attended a dinner hosted by Heath at Kenneth Baker's house the day after the October election loss.

Hurd's diary noted that they discussed everything, except the vital issue of his own fate. "He is healthy but full of anger and reproach towards the press lords, advisers, etc. I insist on a united Opposition. But this isn't the point, and we all know it. I fear that he will sail on to shipwreck.

A sensible wife would have pointed it out that, even if Heath accepted the leadership challenge, it did not result in a positive outcome for him personally. Heath was psychologically incapable to show kindness to natural allies or to complicity to rivals after the two general elections defeats.

According to Tebbit's account there was not much open acrimony among the parliamentary party. "It was a deep sense of despair. What are we going oh?

Tebbit tells a tale from that time as an illustration. Heath had been invited for a dinner by a backbench-dining group. It was a semiformal event in which guests were allowed to ask the guest or honour questions. "I took the straw of immigration. "I stated that a lot people in my constituency were concerned about it so he asked me his thoughts on our current immigration policy."

Heath replied, "I don't want to talk that", to the effect that Tebbit highlighted that it was something that was close to his constituents hearts. Heath repeated his statement, emphatically concluding: "I said no I don't wish to discuss this."

Tebbit's favorite character trait was Heath's sheer rudeness, petulance. I suggested that Heath had a certain grandness when we spoke. Tebbit corrects that I am wrong: "There wasn't a lot of grandness about him."

Thatcher announced her intention to run against Heath and she pursued her campaign with the same determination. She was aware of the intense scrutiny she would be facing, just like Keith Joseph, who was the front-runner. Generally, she was careful with her public statements. An interview she did before the October election for Pre-Retirement Choice was almost fatal. With inflation at 20%, she encouraged readers to follow her example, keep their kitchen cupboards stocked with tinned fruit and fish, and save money. Pre-Retirement Choice readers are her favorite, as her own husband, now 60, was soon to retire from Burmah Oil.

Even though it seemed like simple, homepun advice, it was actually spotted by a Heath loyalist - it is believed to have been Peter Walker - who fed it into national media. A number of pensioners' spokespersons and the National Association of Housewives were persuaded that hoarding was unacceptable. Thatcher, deeply affected by the frenzy, was forced to allow media inspection of her pantry. It was absurd to accuse her of hoarding. Although hoarding was a serious problem during the War, it was not considered patriotic. None of the tinned goods that she found on her shelves were out of stock, even though they were priced higher by retailers each month. She was not safe from this attack, however. It cleverly played into the prejudices within the party against her - that she was a small-bourgeois representative the rentier classes and therefore not fit for leading a great party.

Although she was hurt, she was mentally stronger than her enemies. She told her friends, "Don't underestimate my strength," a few days later.

Heath's foolish decision to transfer Thatcher to the second spot in the shadow Treasury group had started to backfire. She was proving to be a great performer, especially when she was compared with her weak boss, Robert Carr.

In January, she had an open exchange with Denis Healey and condemned what she saw as the terrible consequences of Labour's Capital Transfer Tax. She suggested that many people see making provision for their children "a duty" and "a privilege".

Healey could not resist a Tory spokeswoman using privilege and turned it around in her face. Healey refers to the charismatic communist orator for the Spanish Civil War. He dismisses her as "La Pasionaria."

Healey appeared to be winning the exchange. Labour benches laughed, but Thatcher didn't seem to be on the ropes. She was simply waiting her turn.

She got up and said, "I wish I could claim that the Chancellor was doing himself no less than justice." Unfortunately, I cannot affirm that he had done his job justice. Some Chancellors can be macro-economic. Some Chancellors are macro-economic. This one is just plain inexpensive."

Not only did she place Healey - a well-seasoned Commons bruiser- in his spot, but Labour's attack on her for representing "privilege" somehow reminded Tories how she came from no establishment background. She was unlike the rest of the Tory front bench empty suits. It was important that she would fight back against Labour ministers who wanted to increase taxes on the middle classes. This Commons exchange was the most clear statement that, should she be elected Tory leader it would end the cosy, de-facto consensus between both parties. It brought joy to Tory hearts, even if some men did not agree with what she stood for. Margaret Thatcher would be the Conservative fighter to the Labour government. Nicholas Ridley a Tory MP said, "Here's a senior figure that didn't appear beaten at ALL," years later. "She exuded confidence. She was a convert to many.

Thatcher was being positioned in 1975 as the politician who would lead a nation-wide revival. She was a prelude to Ronald Reagan. Reagan ended the Carter gloom in the Carter years and was able, through his 1984 re-election bid, to boast: "It is morning again in America."

After making the decision to stand in late November, she went to Heath's House of Commons offices. She noted in her autobiography she heard him say "If you have to", although she could recall him saying "You won't lose" (which she claims sharpened her competitive instincts). Heath stated in his memoirs that Heath thanked her, but it is clear that the meeting was arctic.

The date of the first ballot for the leadership elections was February 4, and the Daily Telegraph was used to settle internal party disputes. Although it was disapproving of any leadership coups, the paper did NOT endorse any candidate. WF Deedes was the new editor. He created a rolling section on the paper's leader page, called 'My Kind of Tory Party.' The principal leadership contenders were invited in to contribute. Journalists often create this type of series in times when seismic change is occurring. It is intended to give readers an illusion that their paper is going on to decide the outcome of a contest.

Thatcher's contribution was a punchy statement of middle-class values and an implicit condamnation of Heathite pale hearts. In essence, she demanded that Tories believe in their instincts. She also asked them to stop shilly dancing. "If a

Tory refuses to believe that private property is one bulwark for individual freedom, he might as well become a socialist. In fact, people believe that too many Conservatives became socialists.... Why should anyone vote for a party that seems to have no convictions?" Although her article was intended as an appeal to Britain's voters, it read like a punchy demolition of everything Heath had accomplished in his almost ten years as leader.

*

Heath's attempt to define the Tory party he wanted was published the day before the first vote. It was, according John Campbell, "a parody on woolly centrism" that included vague appeals at moderation, balance, national unity, and other such things.

Thatcher's comments had been an attack against Heath. He repaid the favor, stressing that he believed the promotion and preservation of harmony was a key Tory value. His opponent threatened to subvert it. "This shifting of ours is that we are the despair naive analysts who demand a straightforward answer to the query, 'What' do you stand for?' It may have been a dig at Heath's ghostwriter at Thatcherite pundits. If so it shows how Heath had allowed his own weakness for score-settling to infect his campaign team with devastating consequences that would soon become evident.

Thatcher was defeated by the Conservative establishment. The news broke that Alec Douglas Home had publicly supported Heath one day before the first vote. "As a former

Prime minister and Tory leader who selflessly provided a path for a successor," the Daily Telegraph political correspondent said, "Lord Home is a special place in the affections"

In reality, Home's assumption that Home would swing the party in his favor was just a confirmation of how outlandish and outof touch the "establishment". Even the Daily Telegraph did not support Heath but instead endorsed him on the morning of his first ballot. It predicted Heath's victory and advised him to make amends for his inflexibility, aloofness and tendency to surround himself by like-minded colleagues.

*

Heath's group had been lured into false optimism by Airey Neave's clever tactics. He consistently underplayed Thatcher's chances. Lord Tebbit played an important role in the advancement of Thatcher's campaign under Neave. He recalls that "we knew Margaret was going to do much better than we expected on the first round of voting so we convinced Willie Whitelaw's friend and others that they had to vote for Margaret. It was deceit.

Thatcher campaign faced the challenge of convincing non-Thatcherite MPs in order to get them to vote for her. They assumed that in the second vote, they would be able to vote for a candidate more amiable to them.

"I sold the idea even to Michael Heseltine. Tebbit says that he is certain that he voted on the first ballot for her," although Heseltine has never confirmed it and canvass returns strongly suggest that he abstained.

Neave was able to see that Thatcher would win the first vote convincingly, forcing Heath's resignation. That was how it turned out.

Tebbit says that "a lot of those votes which went for Margaret in this first ballot weren't really for Margaret". "They were to secure another ballot. They were to get rid Heath but not to elect his successor."

Thatcher beat Heath 130 votes to 119. Hugh Fraser was the candidate for Right-wingers that couldn't stomach a women leader on 16. Six abstentions, five spoiled ballot papers and five other votes were recorded.

Heath knew he couldn't hang on. "CAN ANYBODY END HER NOW?", Heath asked the Daily Mail on the following day. They noted that Whitelaw, who had resigned, was free to stand for the second round. Even at that point it was clear that Thatcher had the momentum and that he would suffer for the failure to challenge Heath earlier. The Mail's frontpage photo featured Denis And Margaret Thatcher and Mark Thatcher, who were accompanied by Mark's son, at a champagne party at Airey Narrow's Westminster flat. At the time, some wondered if it was in the best of taste since she had already killed off an important leader, but she hadn't yet inherited the throne.

Airey Neave told Thatcher to go towards the centre as a response to Whitelaw's entry on the second ballot.

Whitelaw was able to use his tactic well and never lost the air of someone who was just going about the motions of trying to find a job.

Thatcher did not stop her tireless campaigning, and her attraction to Tory MPs to her side. She didn't take anything for granted. In the hope of winning, she even thought it might be a fateful decision to have her hair cut on the morning before the second ballot.

She was never an emotional warm mother to her twins. Denis did not share her love of Mark and Carol, so she had an indulgent side to her. Carol was sitting for her legal finals that day, and Margaret could sense her nervousness around the breakfast table.

Carol's account shows that the following awkward exchange happened:

"What's your matter darling?"

"Today's examination mum," I replied.

She laughed and said, "Well you can't feel as nervous as I,"

Carol only learned about her mother's victory after she had completed her three hour exam. After that, the invigilator said there were reporters outside. He led Carol out of the building's back, and Carol returned home to Chelsea as the consequences began to sink.

Whitelaw won the second ballot, winning Thatcher with 146 votes to Whitelaw's score of 79. The balance went to those men who didn't have the courage to take Heath. Margaret Thatcher waited for the results in Neave's small Commons office. "I must inform you that you are the Opposition Leader," he said to her. Later, she recalled how he spoke so quietly.

Douglas Hurd was sitting in the Commons Library, doing some work. The cheers and applauses of the Backbench Thatcher supporter heard him as the results were declared upstairs at Committee Room 14. He said that he has always disliked hearing the sycophantic applause of which the party is so addicted when they are on such occasions. Although they were not political soul-mates he still had respect for Thatcher. He confided in his diary that he knew she was a practical lady who knows the traps.

According to the Daily Mail, some laddish Tory MPs began to chant, according to one reporter.

Knock Knock...

Who's there?

Ted...

Ted who?

You see you've forgotten already.

Her triumphant reaction was unmistakable. MRS. THATCHER ROUTS RIVALS, the Telegraph reported the next day. HB Boyne, the paper's political correspondent - the man who confidently predicted Heath's victory just nine days prior - wrote perhaps one of today's most embarrassing 'intros'.

"A radiant Mrs Margaret Thatcher, 49, wife of a business executive mother of twins made history yesterday by becoming first woman to head a British party,"

Margaret Thatcher was probably not offended by Margaret Thatcher's emphasis on her marital status, motherhood, or casual displays of sexuality. She never liked women who called themselves feminists and rarely took offense at them.

She had more to worry, as the Telegraph leader on the same occasion reminded her after congratulating "bonny fighters" for their success. Given her humble upbringing, she "ought to not suffer, therefore from that fatally and characteristic Tory defect in guilt about wealth" that so often has put the party at disadvantage in its support for capitalism over Socialism.

"Mrs Thatcher must put some heart into us all, beyond attacking the policies implemented by the Labour Government," added the Telegraph's leader. Let her draw on her personal experience to show us that failure does not have to be inevitable. It is possible to use effort, ability, faith and perseverance to make a difference for people and nations. She will then not only be the leader for the Tory Party but for all the unbeaten British people. Disraeli, Churchill and the other shades of Disraeli will then be able to admire the first woman leader for their party with hope.

Margaret Thatcher was hurriedly, but triumphantly, making her way back to

London as the leader went to press. Carol was exhausted from her legal finals and had decided to stay with a neighbour in order to escape the hubbub. Margaret came to visit her daughter who was already half asleep.

Carol later remembered that she "remembered thinking that she instantly looked a part." "She was just returned from a party and the aura that she had of power was almost a halo. As if this was her destiny, she accepted her new position. She wished my good luck with the next exam the day after and then said goodnight. I went to bed confident that the future would never be the exact same.

Carol Thatcher was right about all of that.

II

THE EARLY CHILDHOOD OF IRON LADY

Socialism has the drawback of you eventually running out on other people's money.

Margaret Thatcher

Margaret Thatcher, also known as Margaret Hilda Roberts was born in Grantham (a small market town in southern Lincolnshire), England on 13 October 1925. Beatrice Ethel, and Alfred Roberts were her parents. Alfred was a local farmer and preacher who eventually became the Mayor for Grantham. Margaret was a part of the family grocery business, helping her father and her sister Muriel. Albert, her dad, was active in Grantham's Finkin Street Methodist Church. Beatrice, Beatrice, and Margaret raised Muriel to be faithful Methodists. Margaret lived with her sibling and parents in the apartment above her parent's North Parade grocery shop.

Her father was the Mayor of Grantham from 1945 to 1952. But he lost his position in 1952 when he became alderman to the labor party that had a majority at the Grantham Council. Margaret became a leader after seeing her father achieve leadership positions at a young ages. Her father, a member of the local council, introduced her to conservative politics. It was from him that she learned the conservative mindset which would eventually become a powerful force in British politics.

Margaret always believed in conservatism. She was 12 when she, along with her sister Muriel, set aside their pocket allowances in order to help pay the expenses of a Jewish teenage girl fleeing Germany from the Second World War. Throughout the war, the teenager was provided shelter by her family.

MARGARET THATCHER GOES TO SCHOOL

M

Argaret attended Huntingtower Road Secondary School. In 1936, she won a scholarship to continue education at Kesteven and Grantham Girls School. She demonstrated a strong commitment to her education, which was evident in her school records. She was hardworking and engaged in extracurricular activities including field hockey, piano recitals, poetry recitals, swimming, and walking. Margaret was a strong leader at school and was named Head Girl during the 1942-1943 academic year. She applied to Somerville College at Oxford in order to study chemistry in 1943. Somerville was a college that offered women's education at the time, and rejected her first application. However, they later admitted her after she had withdrawn another applicant.

Margaret studied chemistry at Somerville during 1943-1947. She specialized in Xray crystallography. Her dissertation was on the structure Gramicidin, an antibiotic. Dorothy Hodgkin served as her supervisor. From the beginning, she was not entirely interested in studying chemistry. She only wanted to become a scientist for a time and she also had the ambition to fulfill her lifelong dream to be a visionary political leader. She kept herself updated with current politics and laws while working as a chemical engineer. It was reported that her pride in being the first British prime Minister to have a degree from science was greater than her pride in being the first female prime ministre.

Tony Bray, a young soldier cadet, met her at Oxford. Tony was impressed at her unique enthusiasm for politics, something that was rare among women at the time. Margaret was a favorite of his and he described her father as a "slightly sexier" and "totally accurate" man. He described his mother as "motherly", "very traditional" and "very competent". Tony's military training made it more difficult for Margaret to stay in Oxford. Tony hoped that their relationship would end, as he thought

Margaret had taken it more seriously than he did. Margaret, trying to avoid the question when asked later about Tony Bray, admitted that they both had their own circumstances.

Margaret Roberts (Thatcher), became the Oxford University Conservative Association's president in 1946. She was greatly influenced during her time at the university by Friedrich Hayek (1944), an Austrian-British philosopher, economist, and political writer. Hayek is best known for his struggle for classical liberalism. Margaret was fascinated by "The Road to Serfdom", as it called for economic intervention from government to prevent an authoritarian regime.

She graduated with second-class honors from the University of

California, Berkeley in 1947. After her Oxford program was completed, she moved from Oxford to Colchester, Essex. She worked as a research chemist at BX Plastics. While she worked in Essex, she maintained her political ambition. She refused to let her work get in the way of her ambitions and joined the local conservatism association. She was part the University Graduate Conservative Association representative that attended the party's 1948 conference at Llandudno. Margaret rose to high office in a popular group of grassroots Conservative Party supporters, known as "The Vermin Club". Aneurin bevan made an offensive comment and the group was founded.

III

MARGARET THATCHER MAKES AN ENTRY INTO PUBLIC OFFICE

It's dangerous to stand in middle of the road as you can be knocked over by the traffic on both sides.

Margaret Thatcher

Her first chance at public office was when a friend from Oxford introduced to her the chairman of Dartford Conservative Association, Kent. Officials of the association had been searching for candidates for the coming elections and were so impressed by her, they accepted her application even though her name wasn't on their list. In January 1951, she was chosen and included on the approved roster.

When she was adopted, she attended a dinner in February 1951 as the candidate to Dartford. She met Denis Thatcher who is a successful businessman and wealthy. Denis took her to the station, where she boarded a train to Essex.

Margaret met Denis after Tony Bray, but he wasn't her first encounter with Denis. Willie Cullen, an American farmer, had first met her in 1949. Cullen was a man she liked and she went on many dates with him, but her interest in Muriel being there was greater. She wrote this in one of her letters to Muriel

"I went to the flicks with a farmer friend yesterday and got him ready to meet up sometime. I showed him the photograph of you and me (sic), together, and he said he couldn't discern the difference. When are you available to visit me for a weekend getaway? "

Only a few weeks after Margaret began her relationship with Willie, Muriel came to Colchester. Willie met Muriel while still being interested in the future prime minster. Willie presented Margaret with lavish gifts including a luxurious bag with her initials written on it. The intention was to win her love. Margaret was able, however, to get Willie & Muriel together. The pair were married in 1950.

MARGARET MEETS SIR DENIS FOR THE FIRST TIME

M

argaret Bobs (Thatcher), moved from London to Dartford to get ready for the forthcoming elections. J. Lyons and Co.

provided her with a steady income. Hammersmith: She was a research chemicalist and part of a group that worked on suitable emulsifiers. Margaret knew she couldn't win the Liberal Partys nomination, but she was still determined to make an impact. She won the respect of her peers by her speeches. Margaret attracted media attention because she was both the youngest and the only female representative. Despite twice losing the election to Norman Dodds, her opposition was reduced. During her campaigns, her parents supported her and Denis Thatcher, whom she later married in Dec 1951. Margaret described Denis in one of many letters she wrote her sister Muriel, sharing stories about her romance and forays into politics.

"A Major Thatcher, aged about 36, with lots of money not very attractive creature - very reserved, but quite nice"

Margaret decided to attend the Inns of Court School of Law because she wanted to be able to develop her political ideologies. Her husband Denis supported her studies. Denis, her husband, gave her the opportunity to have twins Mark and Carol. Carol was born prematurely by Denis. Margaret earned her Law degree. After that, she worked as a lawyer and was able to spend more time with her children. She didn't participate in the 1955 general elections. After several years, she decided that it was finally time to get back in politics. After narrowly defeating Ian Montagu Fraser 1958, she was selected by the Conservative Party as their candidate for Finchley.

MARGARET THATCHER BECOMES A MEMBER OF PARLIAMENT

S

After a vigorous campaign in the 1959 general electoral campaigns, he was chosen as a member of parliament to represent Finchley. Margaret in her maiden address supported the Public Bodies Admission to Meetings Act 60, which requires local authorities to meet in public. The bill was passed in law. She voted against the party's bill to reinstate birching as Judicial Corporal Punishment (JCP). This demonstrated that her party was not going to influence her in making decisions about her job. She was considered a potential prime Minister because of her determination and passion, even in her 20s. She quickly denied the possibility and stated that she had been appointed prime minister in 1970.

"There will not ever be a female prime minister in my lifetime. The male population has too many prejudices."

Harold Macmillan elevated her to the frontbench and made her Parliamentary Undersecretary at The Ministry of Pensions and National Insurance. She was among the first to be elected to the Parliament in 1959, and was the youngest woman to reach such a position. After the defeat of the Conservatives in 1964, she was made the spokesperson for land and housing issues. She used this position for her party's plan to permit tenants to buy Council Houses they lived in. She joined the Shadow Treasury in 1966. She was the treasury's spokesperson and opposed Labours income and price caps. She believes they will indeliberately make it difficult to change the economy. Party leaders quickly began to consider Margaret Thatcher a likely Shadow Cabinet member. Jim Prior suggested her to the Shadow Cabinets, but Chief Whip William Whitelaw & Edward Heath agreed that Mervyn Pike should be the Shadow Cabinet's only woman member. She condemned Labour Governments high tax policies at the Conservative Party Conference of 1966 and called them "not only towards Socialism but also towards Communism". She argued that a lower tax discourages hard work. She was also one among few Conservative Members of Parliament that supported David Steels bill to legalize abortion. She also voted for the ban against hare coursing. She voted for capital punishment, but not the reduction in divorce laws.

In 1967, The United States Embassy at London selected Thatcher to participate on a professional exchange program called International Visitors Leadership Program (known as then the Foreign Leader Program). This program allowed her to spend six weeks visiting US cities and institutions, meeting various political figures. One such institution is IMF (International Monetary Fund). Although she was not yet a member in the Shadow Cabinet, the Embassy informed the State Department that she was going to be the next Prime Minister. Margaret Thatcher was able, thanks to this description given by the embassy, to meet with high-ranking people at a busy programme focused on economic issues. Paul Samuelson, Nelson Rockefeller Pierre-Paul Schweitzer, Walt Rostow and Pierre–Paul Schweitzer were some of these high-ranking people. Edward Heath, leader of the party, named Margaret to the Shadow Cabinet in his capacity as spokesperson for fuel and power. Before 1970's general election, she was promoted twice: first as Shadow Transport spokesman, then as Education.

Enoch Powell was a British MP who addressed a gathering at the Conservative Political Centre in Birmingham on 20 April 1968. He spoke out against the Race Relations Bill, which was then being considered, and also the mass migration to the United Kingdom. His speech caused a lot of uproar and was later referred to as the

"Rivers of Blood", due to a quote in it. Powell became immediately the most divisive, and most talked about, politician in the nation. Edward Heath (the Conservatives' party leader) dismissed Powell from his Shadow Cabinet. His comments against immigration led to him being fired. Margaret Recalls how heath told Margaret on the phone that Enoch Powell would be fired. Margaret stated that it was better to have things cool down in the present than to make the crisis worse. She felt his beliefs on Commonwealth immigration were true and that he was being misquoted during his speech.

MARGARET THATCHER EMERGES AS SECRETARY OF STATE

I

In 1970, the Conservative Party won a majority of the general elections and Margaret was reappointed as Secretary of State in Education and Science. Due to attempts by governments to reduce spending, Margaret immediately attracted the attention and resumption her new office. She placed academic needs first and called on the government to reduce administrative public expenditures in the state education system. It led to the elimination of free milk from schools for children aged seven through eleven. She stated that schools would have to charge for milk, but she was willing to give a quarter pint daily to the younger children as a nutrition purpose. Margaret was dubbed "Thatcher The Milk Snatcher" after her decision. Later papers from the Cabinet revealed that

Margaret was opposed the policy but was pressured by the treasury to support it. Labour and the media reacted strongly to her decision not to allow free milk in the schools. Later in her biography she said that she considered quitting politics following the uproar. She explained that she had experienced the most political odium for the minimal amount of political benefit.

Margaret Thatcher fully supported Lord Rothschilds proposal in 1971 for market forces to affect government spending on research. The department investigated the proposal to increase local education authorities to abolish grammar school and to accept comprehensive second-level education. She tried to retain grammar schools and remained committed to the operation of a secondary moderngrammar school system of education in phases. She refused 326 of the three-hundred and twelve2 requests to make schools into comprehensive schools. During her tenure the percentage of pupils who attended comprehensive school increased from 32% a 62%.

Edward Heath, who was the Conservative party leader, helped to form the "Heath Ministry" which was named by Queen Elizabeth II on the 19th of Juni 1970. This came just one day after the general election. Heaths Ministry was challenged by union demands for a rise in wages and an end to oil embargoes. Labour lost the February 1974 general electoral elections and created a minor government. It won the October 1974 general Elections by a narrow majority. As time passed it became unlikely that Edward Heath would continue to lead the Conservative Party. Margaret was initially seen as unlikely to succeed Edward Heath but she emerged later as the likely candidate, promising a fresh start. Heath lost the first round to Margaret, and he was forced to resign as party leader. Whitelaw was defeated in second ballot. Margaret's victory in party leadership elections divided the party. The majority of her support came both from Members of Parliament on the right and those from South England.

THE IRON LADY RULES THE OPPOSITION

M

On February 11, 1975, argaret Itcher became the leader and opposition leader of Conservative Party. Whitelaw was her deputy. Heath had never been supportive of Thatcher's leadership.

Thatcher was a frequent visitor to the Institute of Economic Affairs. (IAE) was founded by Anthony Fisher. Since the 1960s, Shecher was a frequent visitor and avid reader of the IAE's publications. She became a leader in the anti-British welfare state ideology after she was exposed to the ideas of Ralph Harris and Arthur Seldon. They believed Keynesian Economics was a hindrance to Britain's progress. The institute produced pamphlets proposing lower taxes, less government, greater freedom for consumers and businesses.

Gordon Reece advised Thatcher that she work on improving her presentation after being criticised by

Clive James (TV critic). Reece offered Laurence Olivier voice coaching lessons to Thatcher. She was able, at times, to keep her Lincolnshire dialect under control. It was more difficult for her to suppress during stress. This was evident in 1983, when Denis Healey provoked her. She accused the Labour Frontbench of being frit.

Thatcher, the leader in the opposition, was strongly against the creation and operation of a Scottish Assembly. She directed Conservative MPs not vote for the Scotland/Wales bill in December 1976. The bill was ultimately defeated. When new bills were introduced, she supported amendments to the legislation to allow English citizens to vote in the 1979 referendum regarding Scottish devolution.

Britain's 1970s economic crisis was so bad that James Callaghan (foreign secretary) warned his Labour Cabinet colleagues of the potential collapse of democracy. He said that "if you were a young person, I would emigrate." The economy started to recover around 1978 and opinion polls confirmed that Labour was ahead. The general elections were just around the corner, and Labour was likely to win. Many were shocked when Prime Minister Callaghan announced September 7th that there would not have been general elections. However, he offered to vote in 1979, the next year. Thatcher responded by calling Labour government chickens. She was also supported by David Steel, a Liberal Party leader, who accused Labour Party of 'running scared''.

The Labour government was under fire from the public during the winter 1978-1979. Protests and strikes followed, later being called the "winter of discontent". The Labour government's inability or ability to create jobs was challenged by the Conservative party. They used media ads that featured the slogan, "Labour isn't working". In the early 1980s, Callaghan lost the ministry and a motion to no confidence was made. A general election was then called. 44 seats were won by the Conservative Party in the House of Commons. Margaret Thatcher became Britain's first female Prime Minister after the conservative won the majority of seats.

Thatcher spoke out against the Soviet Union in 1976's foreign policy speech. In a story titled "Iron Lady Raises

Fears", Captain Yuri Gavrilov published in the Soviet Army journal, "Krasnaya Zvezda" (Red Star), Thatcher challenged her views. The Soviet Army journal was featured in The Sunday Time of the United Kingdom the day after. Thatcher made reference the publication a week later in a speech she gave to Finchley conservatives. She likened it the Duke of Wellington's nickname "The iron Duke". Thatcher was, however called the "Iron Lady" throughout her political career.

IV

MARGARET THATCHER TAKES ON THE ROLE AS PRIME MINISTER

If I can get my way, I am extremely patient.

Margaret Thatcher

Thatcher arrived in Downing Street as the Prime Minster of Britain on May 4, 1979. She paraphrased Saint Francis' prayer upon her arrival.

"Where there are discord, may there be harmony. Where there is error and confusion, may there be truth. Where there is doubt, let us bring faith. When there is despair, let us bring hope.

Margaret Thatcher did not know, however, that she would stay in office until the 1980s. She would then become the most powerful woman on the planet.

Margaret Thatcher became Prime Minister in Britain during a time when there was increased racial fear. In July 1979, she met with William Whitelaw, the Home Secretary, and Lord Carrington, the Foreign Secretary. They discussed the need to decrease the number allowed to settle in the United Kingdom from 10,000 to less than 10,000.

Thatcher was British Prime Minister. She visited Queen Elizabeth II weekly to discuss governance. There was serious concern about her relationship to the Queen. John Campbell, her biographer and historian of her life, stated that

"One of the most fascinating questions about the phenomena of a woman as Prime Minister was how she got along with the Queen. While their relationship was a perfect match, it is clear that they were not close friends. Two women of similar age, Mrs. Thatcher six months older, occupying the same position at top of social pyramid, one head of government, the second head of state, it was inevitable that they would be in some way rivals. Mrs. Thatcher was inconsistent in her attitude towards the Queen. One side was her almost religious reverence for the monarchy. She always made sure that everyone sat down at the table to watch the Queen's broadcast. However, she was trying simultaneously to modernize her country and eliminate many of its values and practices.

Thatcher wrote:

"I have always found her attitude towards the Government to be absolutely correct... Stories of clashes between two powerful women' were just so good that I couldn't resist."

Thatcher was the leader and influencer of the government's policies. He was also influenced by economists such as

Milton Friedman and Alan Walters. Thatcher and Geoffrey Howe (the Chancellor) reduced direct taxes on income while increasing indirect taxes. Inflation was decreased by increasing interest rates to stop money from growing faster. She set cash limits on public expenditure and reduced spending on social services, such as education and housing. After a 738-319 vote and student petition, she was made the first Oxford-trained postwar Prime Minister without an honorary doctorate.

Thatcher's City Technology Colleges were not successful. This funding agency was set up to monitor expenditures through the closing and opening of schools. It was described to have "an extraordinary range in dictatorial capabilities". Some

Conservatives who were loyal and supportive of Heath voiced doubts about Thatcher's policies. British media debated the necessity for a policy U turn after the 1981 England Riot. Thatcher spoke out on the subject at the 1980 Conservative Party conference. She used phrases that Ronald Millar had written, including the lines-

"You can always turn if it's your choice. The Lady isn't for turning!

Thatcher's job approval rating decreased over time, to 23% by 1980. This was the lowest number for any Prime Minister. She raised taxes when the recession of early 1980s got worse, which was against the concerns expressed by 364 economists in a March 1981 Statement. By 1981 there was evidence of an economic recovery in Britain. Inflation had fallen to 8.6% from 18.% and unemployment was at its highest point since the 1930s. In 1983, there had been a strong economic recovery. Mortgage and inflation rates were at their lowest in 13 years. While manufacturing employment dropped to over 30% as a proportion of total employment, total unemployment was high at 3.3million in 1984.

BRITAIN HAS FOUND A NEW ECONOMIC HERO

B

In 1987, the unemployment rate fell, inflation was low, while the economy was strong. Opinion polls revealed that Conservatives were in control. There was also success at local council elections. Thatcher decided to call for a general vote, which was set for June 11th. Even though the deadline for elections was still 12 months away. Thatcher's Third consecutive term was made possible thanks to the success of Conservatives during the election.

Margaret Thatcher opposed British membership of the Exchange Rate Mechanism. (ERM) was a pioneering institution in the European Monetary Union. She felt that it would reduce the British economy, regardless of the appeals from Nigel Lawson (her Chancellor of Exchequer) and Geoffrey Howe (her Foreign Secretary). Lawson's successor in office as Chancellor convinced her to join ERM at what was believed to be too high of a rate.

Margaret Thatcher made changes in local government taxes. She replaced domestic rates by a new community cost, in which every adult resident was charged the same amount. The new tax policy was introduced first in Scotland in 1989. It was also adopted later in Wales, England and Wales the next year. This was her least popular policy. This led to a march of more than 200,000 people in London in March 1990. The public demonstration at Trafalgar Square caused riots that led to the injury and arrest of 113 persons. John Major, her successor was freed from the community charge in 1991.

Thatcher saw the danger in the trade unions for both the public, and ordinary trade unionists. She wanted to lower the power of the unions that she saw as a threat to both the public and ordinary trade unionists. Numerous unions started to strike in protest of legislation they were trying to weaken. But resistance eventually faded. Only 309% voted Labour in 1983's general election. BBC reported in 2004 that Thatcher had "managed destruction of the power trade unions for almost an entire generation". Margaret Thatcher's 1984-85 miners' strike was the largest confrontation between the unions of the government.

In March 1984 the National Coal Board ("NCB") incited to close 20 of 174 government-owned mining operations and eliminate 20,000 jobs of the total of 187,000. More than half of country's miners were under the control of the National Union of Mineworkers. Scargill refused to allow a ballot to be held on the strike because he had already lost three ballots to a national strike. The High Court of Justice declared Scargill's refusal to hold the ballot illegal.

Thatcher stood firm and refused the union's demands. She compared the dispute with the Falklands conflict to the miner's, something she said in 1984. "We couldn't fight the enemy without going to the Falklands. The enemy within is far more dangerous than liberty and much harder to defeat. After nearly a full year of strike action the NUM leadership finally gave in to demands and signed a March 1985 agreement. The economic impact of the strike action on the economy was nearly PS1.5 billion. The strike action also caused the devaluation of the pound against the dollar. In 1985, the state closed 25 non-profitable coal mines. By 1992, there were 97 coals mines left.

The closure of 150 coalmines, some of them not losing money, caused thousands to lose their jobs and had a devastating impact on entire communities. Thatcher was determined not to let Heath's government down by his strike actions. Thatcher's strategies to win over the striking miners were to prepare fuel stocks, appoint Ian MacGregor the NCB leader, as well as ensure that the police was properly trained and equipped with the right gear to handle riots. When more than 29 million work days were lost in 1979, the UK saw an increase of 4,583 stoppages. The loss of 27 million working day was caused by the 1984 strike of the miner's. There were 1,221 stoppages. During Thatcher's second term, stoppages declined dramatically. In 1990 there were 630 ceasepages, which resulted in less than 2million working days being lost. This number is continuing to fall as the years progress. Thatcher's time as Prime Minister saw a marked decline in the number of trade union members. In 1979, the percentage of workers who belonged to a union was 57.3%, and it dropped to 49.5% in 1985. From Thatcher's 1979 assumption of office until her departure, the number members of trade unites dropped from 13.5million down to less 10 million.

Thatcher was a staunch supporter for privatization. After the 1983 general elections, the sales of government utilities increased. Private privatization of state-owned industries was responsible for more than PS29billion, while sales of council housings brought in another PS18billion. The improvements in productivity and performance in the economy led to the sale of all state industries. Some of the industries that were privatized, including water, electricity, gas, were natural monopolies for which there was not an increase of competition. These industries were subject to increased regulations and laws in order to make up the lost government control. Oftel and Ofgas were established as regulatory bodies. In order to lower the prices of goods and services as well as improve efficiency in privatized sectors, consumers benefited from the privatization of their industries. Thatcher, however was against privatization of British Rail. Nicholas

Ridley, the then Transport Secretary, is reported to have said that.

"Railway Privatization will be the Waterloo this government." Please do not ever mention the railways to my face again.

Before she was forced to resign as Prime Minister in 1990 she had agreed to the privatization of British Rail that John Major, her successor, had implemented in 1994. In order to stimulate economic growth, financial deregulation was also combined with privatizations of state assets. Geoffrey Howe, the UK Chancellor, eliminated exchange controls in 1979. This allowed for more capital investments in foreign markets. Many hindrances to the London Stock Exchange were removed with the sudden deregulation.

In an effort to regain political prisoners whose ranks had been vacated by the Labour government's 1976 heralding Labour government, the Provisional Irish Republican Army of (PIRA), and the Irish Liberation Army of (INLA) in Maze Prison in Northern Ireland went on hunger strike in 1980 and 1981. Bobby Sands initiated the 1981 hunger strike by threatening to fast until death unless prisoners were allowed to be recognized for their living conditions. Thatcher refused a return to the political status of prisoners. The British government stated that crime is crime, but it is not politically motivated. The British government secretly spoke to Republican leaders in an attempt to end the hunger strikes. After Bobby Sands's death, and those of nine other prisoners, the strike was over. Some rights were granted to paramilitary inmates, but no official recognition of their status as political prisoners. The violence in Northern Ireland rose during the time of the hunger strike.

Margaret Thatcher escaped an assassination attempt at her by the IRA in a Brighton hotel on October 12, 1984. Unfortunately, five people were shot dead in the assassination attempt. This included the wife of John Wakeham. Thatcher stayed in Brighton at the hotel as she prepared for the Conservative Party conference. Even though she gave her speech as scheduled and it was revised based on the circumstances, People were more likely to support her decision to continue with the planned conference than she was before. Margaret Thatcher created the Anglo-Irish Inter-

Governmental Council in 1981 with Garret Finch. This forum was set up to be a place for both the Irish and British governments. Thatcher, Fitzgerald, and Garret Fitzgerald signed the Hillsborough Anglo-Irish Agreement four years later, on November 15, 1986. It was the first British Government to give the Republic of Ireland advisory status in the administration of Northern Ireland. Ian Pasley led protesters in Belfast with the slogan "Ulster Says No". The number of protestors was over 100,000 Ian Gow was later assassinated. He resigned as Minister-of-State in the HM Treasury. All 15 unionist Members Of Parliament (MPs), resigned their seats in parliament.

Thatcher was supportive of active climate protection and was a key proponent for the passage of the

Environmental Protection Act 1990. She was also a supporter of the Intergovernmental Panel on Climate Change and of the Hadley Centre for Climate Research and Prediction. She helped include acid rain, climate changes and pollution in British mainstream culture towards the end 1980s. Thatcher demanded a global agreement on climate change in 1989. This she made clear in her September 27, 1988 speech to Royal Society and in her November 1989 speech at the UN General Assembly. She was not certain about the climate change policy, and she resigned as Prime Minister in 1990.

ZIMBABWE IS RESCUED BY THE IRON LADY AFTER RACISM.

L

Thatcher appointed ord. Carrington as Foreign Secretary in 1979. Carrington was the Minister for Defence before being appointed as Foreign Minister. He was also a senior member the party. Lord Carrington attempted to avoid domestic issues and was friendly with Thatcher. First was solving the Rhodesia crisis. Partly, the issue with Rhodesia in the early days was racial. In which the 5% majority of whites was determined to control the prosperous former colony of largely African people, the 5% was intent on governing. This led to a worldwide condemnation of the act. The end of the Portuguese Empire, Africa's Portuguese colonial rule in 1975 meant that Rhodesia's main supporter, South Africa discovered that the country was an liability. Carrington was determined to end the black rule and he reached a compromise at the Lancaster House Conference in December 1979. Abel Muzorewa, Joshua Tongogara, Josiah Tongogara, and the Prime Minister for Rhodesia Ian Smith were all present at the conference. This conference led to the end of Rhodesian bush warfare (also known by the Zimbabwean wars of freedom), and the creation of the new country of Zimbabwe under black rule.

V

MARGARET THATCHER'S INFLUENCES FOREIGN POLICIES

The power is similar to being a lady... If you have the nerve to tell people that you are, it's not true.

Margaret Thatcher

Thatcher's first foreign-policy crisis came at the 1979 USSR invasion of Afghanistan. She condemned the invasion, saying that it revealed the bankruptcy of a faulty strategy and helped to convince some British athletes not go to the 1980 Moscow Olympics. She wasn't an ardent supporter of Jimmy Carter of the United States, who attempted to defuse the USSR using economic sanctions. Britain's economy was unstable, so NATO hesitated cutting trade ties. The Financial Times reported Thatcher's government was secretly supporting Saddam Hussein's military equipment since 1981.

Thatcher was a close friend of US President Ronald Reagan's Cold War strategies. This was due to their collective disbelieve about

Communism. In 1983, Ronald Reagan failed to seek her consent for Grenada's invasion. During her first 12months as Prime Minister she supported NATO's decision to put up US nuclear missile cruise and Pershing II cruise missiles in Western Europe. This enabled the US to station more than 160 cruise bombers at RAF Greenham Common. This sparked a rowdy protest from the Campaign for Nuclear Disarmament. Thatcher bought the Trident submarine nuclear missile submarine from the US in order to substitute Polaris. This cost more than PS12Billion, the same price as at 1996. Thatcher's preference for a defense alliance with the US was obvious in the Westland case of 1985-1986. Thatcher worked with her colleagues to allow Westland to reject Agusta's takeover offer. This was in support of Sikorsky Aircraft's preferred option. Michael Heseltine Secretary of Defence, who had signed the Agusta agreement, resigned.

THE FALKLANDS BE RESCUED BY THATCHER

O

The most powerful military junta in Argentina gave permission for the invasion of South Georgia by the British, on April 2, 1982. This was the beginning of the Falklands War. The subsequent crisis was "a defining moment" of Thatcher's premiership. Harold Macmillian and Robert Armstrong suggested Thatcher set up and directed a small War Cabinet (formally ODSA and Defence committee, South Atlantic) that would oversee the conduct and oversight of the war. By 5-6 April, it had approved and sent a naval taskforce to recapture the islands.

Argentina surrendered in June 14th. Operation Corporate was successful despite the deaths of 255 British servicemen, 3 Falkland Islandersers and HMS Conqueror sinking the cruiser ARA general Belgrano. 649 Argentines were killed in the conflict. Half of these died when the nuclear-powered submarine HMS Conqueror hit and sank the cruiser ARA General Belgrano. Tam Dalyell from Parliament was also criticised for not protecting the Falklands. But, overall, Thatcher was a committed and highly effective war leader. Thatcher's second victory at the 1983 general elections was helped by the "Falklands effect", an economic recovery that started in 1982. Also, Theresa May's disillusionment with her opposition.

Simon Jenkins, Max Hastings and Max Jenkins suggested in 1983 that Thatcher was often called the "Falklands spirits" because of her fondness for the quick decision-making of War Cabinet members over the complicated task of promoting a Peacetime Cabinet government.

SHE SIGNS A TREATY WITH THE CHINESE

I

Thatcher visited China in September 1982 for Deng Xiaoping to discuss the sovereignty and future of Hong Kong. Margaret Thatcher visited China in her first visit to a communist state. She was also the British prime minister who first visited China. During their meeting she demanded the PRC's permission for the British territory to be occupied. Deng maintained that Hong Kong's sovereignty by the PRC was undisputed, but he stated his willingness and readiness to negotiate with the British government. In the end, both governments agreed to keep Hong Kong stable and prosperous. After 2 years of negotiations, Thatcher agreed to sign the Sino-British Joint Declaration (in Beijing) in 1984. It included the agreement that Hong Kong would be handed over in 1997.

THATCHER IS A FENEMY OF APARTHEID

I

In April 1986, she granted US F-111s permission to use Royal Air Force base for the bombing in Libya. This was as a response to the alleged attack on a Berlin discotheque by Libyan bombers. Her decision was not supported by more than three quarters of British citizens according to polls.

It was clear that she was supporting "peaceful negotiations" in order to end apartheid. Thatcher, however, was against the South African sanctions imposed by both the Commonwealth and European Economic Community (EEC). She attempted to keep trade with South Africa intact while persuading the government to abandon apartheid. This meant that she posed as President Botha's friend and asked for him to visit the UK in 1984 despite any demonstrations against his government. Thatcher described the African National Congress, (ANC) as "a typical terrorist group" in October 1987. Nelson Mandela gave Thatcher a commendation when he visited Britain in the five months following his release.

"She is an opponent of apartheid... We have a lot to thank for her."

Thatcher and her cabinet supported the Khmer Rouge's right to keep their UN seat, even though they were forced from power by the Cambodian–Vietnamese War. Although Thatcher refused to agree, it was later discovered that the SAS had secretly instructed the CGDK members to train against the Kampuchea(PRK) government. Non-communists like the Khmer People's National Liberation Front or the Sihanoukists were subjugated by the Khmer Rouge, militarily as well. According to Rae McGrath's report, they were trained by the SAS to use booby traps and improvised explosives devices. They also learned how to create and use time delay devices.

Thatcher and her party had supported British membership to the EEC in the 1975 nation referendum. However, Thatcher felt that the organization's power should be restricted in order to ensure free trade. She was also worried that the EEC's methods would contradict her support for smaller government and deregulation. Her resistance towards further European integration became even more apparent during her premiership. This was especially true after her third victory at 1987's general election. In a speech she made in Bruges, 1988, she described her disapproval at the EEC's proposal for a federal structure, and a higher centralization of decision making. She stated, "We haven't succeeded in rolling back Britain's frontiers, only for them to be reimposed at European levels, with a European supra-state exercising new dominance from Brussels."

Margaret Thatcher was among the first Western leaders who reacted kindly to Mikhail Gorbachev's reformist USSR leader. Taken into account the Reagan/Gorbachev summits and the USSR reforms, she declared in 1989 that "We are not in any Cold War now" but that we were in a new relationship "much wider than the Cold War ever existed". She made a 1984 state visit to the USSR and met with Gorbachev (chairman of Council of Ministers Nikolai Ryzhkov).

Thatcher was in America on a working trip when Saddam Hussein attacked Kuwait. She suggested an intervention at her meeting with President George

H. W. Bush in 1989. Bush was prompted to send troops to the Middle East for the pursuit of the Iraqi Army out Kuwait. Bush was cautious about the plan. Thatcher, however, said to him in a telephone conversation that "This is no time for us to go wobbly!" Thatcher's government sent forces to the international Coalition in the final stages of the Gulf War. She had resigned before conflict began on 17th January 1991. She was a backbencher for the coalition's victory, but she warned that "the victories and peace will take more time than the wars." Later it was revealed that Thatcher encouraged Saddam to use chemical weapons against him following the attack in Kuwait.

Thatcher shared the fears of President Francois Mitterrand and was initially against German reunification. Gorbachev said that it "would result in a change to the postwar borders, which we cannot allow because such a development will undermine the stability and threaten our security." She voiced her concerns about a united Germany that would prefer to be part of the Soviet Union rather than NATO. Thatcher was told by Helmut Kohl in March 1990 that he would keep him "informed" about his plans for unification. He also stated that he was available to tell her things that his cabinet might not know. Thatcher celebrated the fall and liberation of the Berlin Wall in November 1989.

PUBLIC RATING DECLINES OF THATCHER

T

Sir Anthony Meyer was a Conservative Party leader candidate and hatcher was a backbench MP who lost support in the 1989 leadership elections. 314 of the 374 Conservative MPs that were eligible to vote voted for Thatcher, and 33 for Meyer. Her followers in the party viewed the result as a success. They were opposed to suggestions that the party was unhappy.

Thatcher was British Prime Minster during her time. She received the lowest approval rating (40%) among post-war Prime ministers. The popularity of her party increased after the resignation in October 1989 of Nigel Lawson, who was the Chancellor. Thatcher was a self-described passionate politician. She maintained that her ratings at polls didn't matter to her and that she was more comfortable with her unbeaten election record.

Opinion polls in September 1990 revealed that Labour Party had taken a 14% lead over Conservatives. And by November, the Conservatives were closely following Labour for 18 more months. These ratings and Thatcher's aggressive personality that tends to dominate college opinion contributed to dissatisfaction within Conservative parties.

Geoffrey Howe was removed as Foreign Secretary by Thatcher after Lawson coerced his wife to accept a plan that would have allowed Britain to join the European Exchange Rate Mechanism. In October 1990, Britain was admitted to the ERM. Howe was the last member of Thatcher's initial 1979 cabinet. He resigned as Deputy Prime Minster on November 1, 1990. His resignation was likely due to Thatcher's open resentment towards plans toward European Monetary Union. Howe made a comment on Thatcher's openly dismissive reaction to the government's suggestion for a new European money that could challenge established currencies ("a hard ECU"), in his resignation speech of November 13.

VI

MARGARET THATCHER RESIGNS AS PRIME MINISTER

To win a fight, you might have to fight it more than once.

Margaret Thatcher

Thatcher's reign of Prime Minister was ended swiftly by Howe's resignation.

Michael Heseltine made a bid to become the Conservative Party's leader on November 14th. Opinion polls had indicated that he would be able to give the Conservatives an advantage over Labour in polls. Heseltine, despite Thatcher winning the first ballot by a vote 204 to152 with 16 abstentions (204 to 152) had sufficient support to force the second ballot. Thatcher had to win a majority, which was at least equal or greater than 15% of 372 Conservative MPs, to win the leadership elections. While she won with 54.8% of the vote, Haseltine received 40.9% and Thatcher needed four votes to win by a margin equal to 15%. Thatcher made it clear that she would fight for the second ballot. But, after consulting her cabinet members and associates, she was convinced to withdraw. After speaking with world leaders, She resigned her role as Prime Minister after meeting with Queen Elizabeth II. She apparently considered her resignation from Downing Street a betrayal when she left. Her resignation shocked many people outside of Britain. Foreign observers Henry Kissinger, Gorbachev and others discreetly expressed concerns.

Thatcher was overthrown by John Major, the Chancellor of the Exchequer and Prime Minister. Heseltine was defeated in the subsequent ballot. Major led the Conservative party to its fourth consecutive victory on March 9, 1992. This was after a 17-month improvement in Conservative support. Major was supported by Thatcher, but his support dwindled as time passed.

After her resignation from the premiership Thatcher became a constituent parliamentarian to become a member on the backbenches. Her domestic approval rating improved following her resignation. The public felt that her leadership had been an asset for the country. At the age 66, she decided to retire from the House after the 1992 general election. She claimed that her departure from Commons would allow her more freedom of speech.

SHE IS STILL A FORCE to RECKON WITH

A

Thatcher was the first prime minister to establish a foundation. After she left the House of Commons in 1993, Thatcher also became the House of Commons' last speaker. In 2005, however, the British wing of Margaret Thatcher Foundation collapsed. She wrote two volumes of memoirs: The Downing Street Years (1993), The Path to Power (1995). Sir Denis Thatcher, her husband moved into Chester Square in 1991. Chester Square is a residential area in Belgravia.

Thatcher was hired by Philip Morris in July 1992 to be a "geopolitical adviser" and paid $250,000 annually to her foundation. Thatcher received $50,000 for each speech she delivered.

In August 1992, she requested NATO to stop Serbian attacks against Gorazde/Sarajevo in order to end the bloodshed from the Bosnian War. She described Bosnia-Herzegovina's situation to "the worst excesses the Nazis" and said that it could lead "to a holocaust". She was completely supportive of Croatian and Slovenian autonomy. Thatcher was interviewed by Croatian Radio-television in 1991 about the Yugoslav Wars. It was her opinion that the Western governments had refused to recognize the Yugoslav Wars as an independent state and failed to arm them after the invasions of the Serbian-led Yugoslav Army.

She spoke in several speeches at the Lords against the Maastricht Treaty. A. V. Dicey was cited when she argued that because all three main parties were in favor of the treaty the people should vote in a referendum.

Thatcher was named honorary chancellor of College of William & Mary in Virginia, 1993-2000. From 1992 to 1998, Thatcher also served as chancellor of University of Buckingham (a private university she opened in 1976 during her time as Education Secretary).

Tony Blair's victory as Labour Party leader in 1994 was acknowledged by Thatcher, who said Blair was "probably" the most formidable Labour leader ever since Hugh Gaitskell. However, Thatcher also stated that she saw "a lot" of socialism behind Blair's front bench. I believe he truly has moved. "Blair replied in a similar manner, saying "She was a thoroughly determined individual, and that's an admirable trait."

Thatcher was vocal in her demand for Augusto Piochet to be freed from Chile. In 1998 Spain had him arrested and was about to charge him with violating human rights. She also mentioned his assistance to Britain during the Falklands War. She visited him in 1999 after he was placed under house detention near London. Pinochet was eventually released in March 2000 by Jack Straw, the then Home Secretary.

Thatcher, like in 1992 and 1997, backed the Conservative campaign at the general election. In the leadership election of Conservative party, following its loss, Thatcher supported Kenneth Clarke over Iain Duncan Smith. She supported George W. Bush to make Iraq a "finished business", and she praised Blair for his "strong, brave leadership" during the Iraq War.

In her Statecraft: Strategies for a Changing Planet, which was published in April 2002, she addressed the same issue. Ronald Reagan committed it to her. Her book mentioned that Israel had to trade land for peace, that the European Union (EU), was a "fundamentally nonreformable", a "classic utopian plan, a monument the vanity of intellectuals and a program that inevitably leads to failure." She suggested that Britain review its EU membership terms. Or, it could leave the EU altogether and become a member in good standing of the North American Free Trade Area.

MARGARET THATCHER EXITS PUBLIC DUTIES DUE TO HEALTH ISSUES

A

After suffering several small strokes, doctors told her not to engage in any more public speaking. She needed to be able to focus on her overall health. She announced in March 2002 that, on advice from her doctors she would not be speaking at any public events and she would cancel any planned speaking engagements.

Sir Denis Thatcher died in June 2003. Margaret Thatcher was cremated.

Thatcher attended, against the wishes of her doctors on June 11, 2004, the state funeral ceremony for Ronald Reagan. Because of her health condition, she had recorded her eulogy several months in advance. Thatcher, along with the Reagan entourage, traveled to California to attend the Ronald Reagan Presidential Library Memorial Service and Interment Ceremony.

Thatcher was critical of the 2005 decision to attack Iraq, two years after it had been made. Although she still supported Saddam Hussein's decision to expel him from power, she stated that as a scientist she would always be searching for evidence and facts before directing the armed forces. On October 13, She celebrated her 80th birthday at the Mandarin Oriental Hotel in Hyde Park. Tony Blair and other dignitaries were also present. Lord Geoffrey Howe was also present. He softly spoke out about Thatcher, saying that

"Her real triumph was to not only transform one party but also two, so that Labour's eventual return would bring about the irreversible loss of that large portion of Thatcherism."

Carol Thatcher's mother was diagnosed with dementia by her daughter in 2005. Carol stated that her mother couldn't remember the beginning of a sentence because her memory loss had caused her to lose her ability to read. Carol wrote in 2008 that her mother was unable to remember the beginning and end of sentences. Later she told how she discovered her mother's dementia by having Thatcher fail to recall the Falklands or Yugoslav wars in conversation. She also mentioned the pain of constantly reminding her mother that Sir Denis Thatcher had died.

Thatcher was present in Washington, D.C., to remember the official Washington, D.C. memorial for the fifth anniversary, September 11 attacks. As Vice President Dick Cheney's guest, Thatcher met Condoleezza and US Secretary of States Condoleezza. Margaret Thatcher, Britain's first prime minister alive in February 2007, was presented with a statue by the Houses. The bronze statue, which stands in front of Sir Winston Churchill, is presented to Margaret Thatcher. She was present on February 21, 2007.

"I might have liked iron - but bronze is fine. It won't rust."

Thatcher was a public backer of the Prague Declaration on European Conscience and Communism and also the Prague Process. He sent a public note of support to its earlier conference.

THE THATCHER'S HELTH DETERIORATES

A

Thatcher suffered a heart attack after she collapsed during a dinner at House of Lords. When she fell on her arm,

Thatcher was again taken to the hospital. Thatcher returned to 10 Downing street in November 2009 to receive an official portrait by Richard Stone. It was a remarkable recognition for a living former Prime Minster. Richard Stone was originally contracted to paint portraits on behalf of Queen Mother and the Queen.

Thatcher was to attend a ceremony to inaugurate a Ronald Reagan statue at the US Embassy in London. However, her illness prevented her from attending. Her last appearance at a sitting of House of Lords was July 19, 2010. On July 2011, the House of Lords announced her resignation. Thatcher was the most competent Prime minister of the past 30 year in an Ipsos MORI Poll before her office closed in July.

Baroness Margaret Thatcher died April 8, 2013, after succumbing to a stroke. After finding it difficult with the staircase at her Belgravia Chester Square residence, she moved into a suite at London's Ritz Hotel. Her death certificate lists the primary causes as a "repeated, transient ischaemic attacks" and "cerebrovascular accidents", while the secondary causes are dementia and a carcinoma of bladder.

The shock news of her passing was met with mixed reactions throughout the UK. There were many tributes in her honor, remembering her as Britain's most prominent and peaceful Prime Minister. Public celebrations were held to honour her death and to commemorate all that she did for Britain during her Premiership.

Thatcher had provided her family with the details of her funeral before her death. Margaret Thatcher was buried with full military honors. A church service took place at St Paul's Cathedral on April 17.

Queen Elizabeth II of England and the Duke Of Edinburgh attended her funeral. It was the second time that the Queen had been at a funeral for any of her former prime minsters. The first was Sir Winston Churchill's state funeral in 1965, with Thatcher present.

Margaret Thatcher's corpse was later cremated at The Mortlake Crematorium. It took place after the St Paul's Cathedral Memorial Service. A service was held in memory of Thatcher at the All Saints Chapel of the Royal Hospital Chelsea's Margaret Thatcher

Infirmary on September 28th. Thatcher's cremains were placed on the hospital grounds in close proximity to her husband Sir Denis Thatcher.

VII

THE THEORY OF THATCHERISM & EFFECTS ON THATCHER'S POLICIES

Now plan your work for today, tomorrow and every day. Next, work your plan.

Margaret Thatcher

Thatcherism was a term that described a major and widespread change in post-war consensus. This included the acceptance by the major political parties of key themes such as Keynesianism (the welfare state and close management of the economy), Keynesianism (the welfare state) and

Thatcherism. Thatcher had promised that the National Health Service "safe in their hands" in 1982. Keith Joseph was an early influence and the term Thatcherism was used later to describe her policies and her personal style.

Thatcher talked about her political beliefs in a key, divisive split with Edward Heath's one nation conservatism and her Conservative forerunners in an interview. It was published in Woman's Own magazine just three months after the 1987 general Election.

"I feel we have gone through an era when too many children are being taught that "I have problem, it is up to the government to solve it!" "I have problems, and I will seek a grant for it!" "I am homeless. I need to be housed by the government!" And so they cast their problems on society. Who is society? There is nothing such as it! There are individuals, families, and there is no government that can do anything but people. It is our duty and obligation to look after us and our neighbor.

While Prime Minister, the percentage of adult shareholders grew from 7 percent up to 25 percent. In addition, more than a quarter million families were able purchase their council houses. This represents a 56% to 67% increase in owner-occupiers since 1979 to 1990. The homes were sold at a discount between 33-55% and 55%, which resulted in large profits for some new home owners. Real estate wealth rose by 88% in the 1980s due to a rise in house prices, and increased earnings.

The market value of shares in privatized utilities was reduced to ensure wide and quick sales rather than capitalizing on national income.

Thatcher's tenure in office as Prime Minister included periods of high unemployment. Some critics on the opposition political spectrum blamed Itcher's economic procedures for the unemployment rate. Thatcher's monetarist economic policies and mass unemployment remained unchanged for decades. This caused social problems such drug abuse and family conflicts, but Thatcher was not responsible. While unemployment did not drop more than its 1979 level under her premiership, the June 1990 rate (5.4%) was less than the April 1979 rate (5.5%). It remains to be seen what long-term impacts her policies on the manufacturing sector will have.

Thatcher stated in Scotland, April 2009 that she didn't regret making the decision to introduce poll tax. Thatcher also decided to end subsidies to "outdated industries" which were in "terminal decline". This was to prevent "the culture of dependence", which has caused such severe damage to Britain. Susan Strange, a political economist noted that the new model for financial growth was called "casino capitalism". This is consistent with her belief in the importance of speculation and financial trade to the economy.

Opposition critics call her troublesome. They claim she tolerated selfishness and greed. Rhodri Morison, a Welsh politician has described Thatcher's character as "overwhelming". Michael White, who wrote in the New Statesman questioned the idea that her policies had produced a net income. Others see her methods as "a mixed basket" or "Curate's eggs".

Thatcher did "little" to advance the cause of women in politics, either within her party nor the government. Burns stated some British feminists viewed her as an enemy. June Purvis stated that Even though Thatcher had fought tirelessly against the sexist injustices her generation faced, she was not willing to make it easier for others to achieve the same heights. Thatcher didn't view women's rights as something that needed special attention. She did not believe, particularly during her premiership. Although she believed that women should be allowed to attend all public appointments by default, Shecher once suggested that people with young children be allowed out of the workforce in order to give them the time they need to take care and manage their children.

Thatcher's concept of immigration in 1970 was part of an increasingly racist public discussion. Martin Barker, film critic, described it as "new racism". Thatcher assumed that the National Front was winning large support among Conservative voters, and warned of immigrant floods. Her goal was to destroy the Front narrative and assert that many Front voters had serious problems that needed to be addressed. Thatcher criticised Labour's immigration policy in January 1978 to win voters over to the Conservatives.

This was followed by a rise of Conservative support, to the detriment the Front. Critics within the opposition responded by accusing her that she was supporting racism. Dave Russell and Mark Mitchell both sociologists responded to Thatcher's accusations of being racist. They claimed that Thatcher's race had been misunderstood. Both major parties took the same stand on immigration policy in her time as Prime Minster of Britain. They passed the British Nationality Act 1981 with bipartisan support. Thatcher didn't mention race in any of the major speeches she gave during her reign as prime minister.

Many of Thatcher's policy ideas influenced the Labour Party. It returned to power in 1997, under Tony Blair as the premier. Tony Blair transformed the party into "New Labour" when it was formed in 1994. This was to expand its outlook beyond the usual supporters and to draw those who had supported Thatcher (e.g. the "Essexman"). Thatcher had stated that the New Labour Party was her greatest achievement.

Alex Salmond, the Scottish First minister, said that Thatcher's agendas had led to the "unintended result" of supporting Scottish independence. Lord Foulkes was adamant that Thatcher had given the momentum for devolution. Thatcher strongly opposed devolution, writing for The Scotsman. She claimed that it would ultimately lead Scottish independence

Thatcher was British Prime minister for 11 years 209 days. This made her longest serving Prime Minister after Lord Salisbury. Her Premiership lasted 13 Years and 252 Days. Lord Liverpool's 14-year-and-305 day tenure in office was the longest. Her tenure as Prime Minister was the longest. This title was not officially recognized until 1905, when the order of superiority gave it recognition.

VIII

MARGARET THATCHER'S RECOGNITIONS

I'm always happy to cheer myself up if someone attacks me personally. It means that they don't have a single argument.

Margaret Thatcher

With more than 40 millions votes cast for the Conservative Party between

1979 and 1987, she has led her party three times to victory at the general elections. The Independent and major newspaper publications hailed her victory in the final election as an "historic hat-trick".

Thatcher was named the fourth-greatest PM of the 20th century by a poll which was conducted by 139 academics. In the BBC poll 100 Greatest Britons 2002, she was ranked first among living persons. Time magazine in 1999 named Thatcher as one the 100 most significant people of the twentieth century. Scottish Widows was a leading financial services company that asked her to lead a poll. Thatcher was named the most influential female of the two century in 2015. In 2016, Thatcher topped BBC Radio 4's Woman's Hour Power List. This list identifies women who have had the greatest impact on women's lives over the past 70 year.

Margaret Thatcher was elected a member of the Privy Council (PC) in 1970 when she was appointed Secretary for State for Education and Science. On her accession to full membership rights, she was the first female honorary member of Carlton Club.

Thatcher was awarded two honorary distinctions during the time she was premiership.

* Invited to be Honorary Fellow of FRIC, Royal Institute of Chemistry on October 24, 1979

* Elected Fellow in the Royal Society (FRS), an issue that caused controversy

among some Fellows of the Royal Society on July 1, 1983

* Ribbon bars

* Ribbon of Merit

* United Kingdom Order of Merit (1990).

* Ribbon of Good Hope

* South Africa Order of Good Hope (1991).

* Ribbon of Presidential Medal of Freedom

* United States Presidential Medal of Freedom (1993).

* Ribbon of the Order of the Garter

* United Kingdom Order of the Garter (1995).

Thatcher was appointed Member of The Order of Merit (OM), by Queen Elizabeth II, in December 1990, approximately two weeks after her resignation. During the ceremony her husband Denis was given a hereditary title baronetcy. Thatcher was the wife of a knight and was therefore allowed to use the honorific "Lady" title, which she refused to do so. When she was granted the title of Lady Thatcher in 1992, she accepted the honor.

In 1999, the United States and South Africa awarded Thatcher the highest civilian honors:

* President George H. W. Bush's Presidential Medal of Freedom, March 7, 1991

* President F. W. de Klerk was presented with the Grand Cross of Order of Good Hope

* Margaret Thatcher Day has been observed in Falkland every January 10, 1992. In commemoration of her first visit, in January 1983. This was 6 months after the Falklands War ended.

Thatcher was appointed a member of House of Lords, earning her the title of Baroness Thatcher of Kesteven (County of Lincolnshire) in 1992. Thatcher was allowed to have her own coat and arms while she was a Baroness. Thatcher received another coat of arm after being made Lady Companion of the Order of the Garter(LG) in 1995. This is the highest order of chivalry women can receive. Thatcher, who was permitted to use her own arms but not allowed to use the Royal Arms as per protocol, occasionally used the Royal Arms.